Praise for *Transcending Loss*

"Dealing with a death in the family ⟨...⟩ world is awful. There is no advice, no ⟨...⟩ it better. But now there is a book to ⟨...⟩ rest of the experience understandable ⟨...⟩ a superbly researched and written guide ⟨...⟩ the tragedies none of us can avoid."

—Jim Lehrer

"For anyone who has suffered a tragic loss, grieving is a life-long process. This compassionate, poignant and practical guide begins where *How to Survive the Loss of a Love* leaves off—the long-term adaptation to major loss. Ashley Prend shows you how to transform lingering darkness and despair into love and light. *Transcending Loss* will be a great blessing on your lifetime journey of recovery."
        —Harold H. Bloomfield, M.D., psychiatrist and author of
        How to Survive the Loss of a Love and
        How to Heal Depression

"What a magnificent gift to those who are experiencing grief and to others seeking that depth of emotional understanding. Ashley Davis Prend will bring transcending inspiration and perceptive insights to many grieving hearts."
        —Rabbi Earl A. Grollman, D.D., author of
        Living When a Loved One Has Died

"Ashley Prend has given an essential gift to those who grieve: a sense of community. *Transcending Loss* offers those who mourn and those who counsel them a guiding hand and compassionate voice. This book is more than a 'how-to'; it is a best friend."
        —Barbara L. Ascher, author of *Landscape Without Gravity:
        A Memoir of Grief*

"Ashley Prend's book moves us beyond a discussion of coping with loss to a much larger perspective on the ways that we live with and transcend grief. It is a very special and sensitively written book that would be valuable to both the bereaved and those that work with them."
        —Kenneth J. Doka, Ph.D., author of *Disenfranchised Grief*
        and editor of *Death and Spirituality*

(continued . . .)

"*Transcending Loss* is a book that provides an inspiring model for any one of us who has suffered a loss of any kind. To transcend loss means to grow from the experience—as awful, as painful, as gut-wrenching as it is—but to use this pain as a means to gather strength, to hope once again that life holds meaning. Prend has punctuated her work with sensitive and loving examples as she gently pulls us through the many problems of grieving. She shows us a spiritual pathway that ultimately leads to healing, transforming the nightmare of grief into a place of strength and new energy. This book guides one through the darkness of bereavement and lifts one lovingly onto a new beginning."
—Catherine Sanders, Ph.D., author of *Surviving Grief . . . and Learning to Live Again*

"Compassionate, eloquent, but above all honest, Ashley Prend has written as helpful a book on grief as any I know. *Transcending Loss* is a wonderful gift both for us and our loved ones."
—Forrest Church, author of *LIFE LINES: Holding On (and Letting Go)* and *God & Other Famous Liberals*

"A guide in our journey through the valley of the emotions of death. *Transcending Loss* treats reactions that could otherwise provoke self-hatred and guilt as a natural part of that journey. The deeper our journey the more we—like a bone broken—can heal stronger than we were before. No one needs *Transcending Loss* more than men, the sex ten times more likely to commit suicide after the death of their spouse. So if someone you love is 'taking it like a man,' buy him—or her—*Transcending Loss* and, well, read it to them."
—Warren Farrell, Ph.D., author of *The Myth of Male Power* and *Why Men Are the Way They Are*

Transcending Loss

Understanding the Lifelong Impact of Grief and How to Make It Meaningful

Ashley Davis Prend, A.C.S.W.

BERKLEY BOOKS, NEW YORK

This book is an original publication of The Berkley Publishing Group.

TRANSCENDING LOSS

A Berkley Book / published by arrangement with
the author

Printing History
Berkley trade paperback edition / August 1997

The Penguin Putnam Inc. World Wide Web site address is
http://www.penguinputnam.com

ISBN: 0-425-15775-X

BERKLEY®
Berkley Books are published by The Berkley Publishing Group,
a division of Penguin Putnam Inc.,
375 Hudson Street, New York, New York 10014.
BERKLEY and the "B" design
are trademarks belonging to Penguin Putnam Inc.

Printed in the United States of America

10   9   8   7

To my Muse,
whose inspiration sustained me along the journey

ACKNOWLEDGMENTS

Writing this book has been a remarkable, blessed journey. From beginning to end, this project was never a solitary venture. Although the process took me to private places of the heart and spirit, it connected me with others who helped bring this book into existence as well. First, I gratefully acknowledge my editor, Denise Silvestro, and all of the wonderful people at Berkley Books, who helped give birth to this book. Denise shepherded the manuscript from proposal to final form with unfailing enthusiasm, insight, and support. She ultimately gave this book a public life, believing in its message from the very start. To her, I extend my deepest thanks.

I also am profoundly grateful to my literary agent, Faith Hamlin, whose unflagging support, sage advice, and dogged persistence kept this book alive. Her unwavering belief in this project helped bring it to fruition. I thank the late Diane Cleaver for first seeing the book's potential and then recommending me to Faith. And I thank Sharon Sakson, wherever you are, for sending me to Diane.

Professionally I have been fortunate to have the overwhelming support of many people and organizations. My colleagues at the Center for Marital and Family Therapy provided me with the freedom to pursue my goal and the flexibility to attain it. Downtown Professional Consultants provided me with the ideal contemplative space in which inspiration could flourish. Also, I extend a special thanks to the dedicated staff of the Supportive Care Program at St. Vincent's Hospital, in particular to my esteemed colleague and friend Kathleen Perry, whose enthusiastic support has been especially meaningful.

I was lucky enough to receive a great deal of writing support, particularly during the conception of this project, from many people. Charles Salzberg, teaching a course at the Writer's Voice, was an early supporter and enthusiast as he helped guide my work. I have appreciated all his influence and advice, both as a writer and as a friend. I also thank the individuals in my writers' group who at various times provided helpful comments and direction, including Yvonne Conde, Maggie Doctor, Nancy Ebker, Julia James, Alexis Sinclair, Lorraine Kriegel, Larry Levine, Andre Moore, Sara Slagle, the late Sabina Wedgewood, and Denis Woychuck. I wish each of them luck with their own works.

Two brave and giving souls read drafts of the manuscript and provided invaluable comments and insights. I gratefully thank Peyton Lewis and Eliza Rossman. They each took it upon themselves to painstakingly provide me with their insights and impressions.

Personally I have been blessed with supportive and thoughtful friends and family who lived this book with me. A special thanks to my mother, who was gracious in her support and who, as a writer herself, provided me with the genetic gift of written communication skills. Thanks also to my father, for his constant encouragement, his proud support, and all those helpful clippings! And I note a very special appreciation to my beloved husband, David. David perhaps better than anyone else knows all that went into this book. He was my cheerleader, my commiserator, my first reader, my informal editor, and my steadfast sustainer, thus providing me with a solid emotional base from which to work. To him, I offer my thanks and my love.

And simply, I could not have written this book without the generous contributions of the fifty individuals who, through interviews, shared their personal, and at times professional, insights about loss. These people graciously, candidly opened their hearts to me in the hope of helping others who grieve. To that end, they are all transcenders of loss, and I thank each of them for the lessons they taught me.

Finally, I could not close without acknowledging you, the reader, and all those who have loved and lost. I wish you strength on your journey through the valley of the shadow, and I wish you inspiration on your journey toward Transcendence.

CONTENTS

Part IV: Roadblocks and Detours to Transcendence

Part V: Getting Back On Track

INTRODUCTION

*When one door closes, another opens, but we often
look so long and regretfully upon the closed door,
we do not see the ones which open for us.*
—ALEXANDER GRAHAM BELL

One of the most striking, and perhaps even most appealing, features of soap operas is that the characters never seem to be permanently scarred by their past tragedies. They live through illnesses, miscarriages, adultery, multiple divorces, and deaths, but the next year, they move on to the next story line seemingly unscathed. Occasionally they refer to the past, but the characters never seem to be too deeply affected or traumatized by it. People even die and miraculously come back to life—sometimes it was all just a dream. We're willing to suspend disbelief because the fiction is so satisfying, so comforting, so unlike real life.

In the real world, tragedies and losses affect us deeply and profoundly. We may eventually move on to a new story line, so to speak, but we do not forget the past and we certainly do not remain unscarred. Our losses affect us irrevocably. When a loved one dies, the deepest loss of all, a part of us dies too and life will never, ever be the same again. That's the bad news. But our grief also has the potential to be transformative, leading to unprecedented levels of psychological and spiritual growth. That's the good news.

Grieving is one of the most universal of all human experiences, cutting across race, nationality, gender, and socio-economic strata. The vast majority of us will outlive our grandparents, our parents, our pets, and some of our friends. Many of us will also outlive our spouses, siblings, and sadly, even our children. Although grief is something we all must encounter eventually, talking about it, ironically, is still one of our great taboos. We can talk about diseases, social ills, politics, and even sex—especially sex. We've even become more comfortable talking about death and suicide, albeit grudgingly. But when it comes to grief, and addressing the ongoing, long-lasting feelings of those who are left in death's wake, we just don't want to face it and we certainly don't want to talk about it.

One griever told me that three years after her twenty-eight-year-old daughter died unexpectedly, she was having a bad day and found herself quite depressed and sad. She called a friend hoping to find a sympathetic ear but instead was assaulted by the friend's exclamation, "You mean you're still grieving over her, after *three years?*" The friend's question was not meant to be malicious. She honestly didn't understand that to a grieving mother three years is nothing. She was sadly ignorant that major loss lasts a lifetime.

This woman is not alone in her ignorance. I've heard educated people tell me that they thought the average length of the grieving process was two to four weeks. Maybe that was just their wishful thinking. We're an immediate-gratification society that values quick fixes, a generation raised on microwaves and fast foods. We prefer our solutions and emotions conveniently packaged for the swiftest consumption. So we expect grief to be a quick and easy process with no bitter aftertaste. But how can we expect to love someone, lose someone—and not be changed irrevocably? How can we realistically expect this to be a speedy process? Yet time and again grievers tell me they are being asked, "When will you be your old self again?" or "It's been three months already, shouldn't you be over this by now?" Perhaps you've heard comments like this too, and chances are that as a result, you feel quite confused and isolated in your grief.

Maybe you've been asking yourself the same questions. Let's face it, most everyone facing grief's darkest days and nights is hungry for relief. In my practice as a psychotherapist and grief counselor, I often hear brave souls wondering "When will this be over?" And I often see people who are in pain many years after the loss berating themselves for their ongoing grief. They ask, "Is it normal to still be hurting so many years later? Is it possible that grief lasts so long?"

The reality is that it is absolutely normal to be still grieving, to still feel the aftershocks of loss for the rest of your life. Grief changes through the years, but the simple truth, which no one wants to admit, is that you will never be your old self again. You are forever changed. That's not to say that you won't heal, because you will find ways to heal. And yes, the raw, jagged pain of acute grief will fade. But just as a very deep wound leaves a lasting scar, you will have an emotional scar that will, at times, still feel sore.

Grieving is not a short-term process; it's not even a long-term process; it's a *lifelong* process. "Having a future" now means that although your life will flow again, it will flow differently as a result of the loss. Your grief will become incorporated into your life history, become a part of your identity. And you will continue now, and forever, to redefine your relationship with your deceased loved one. Death doesn't end the relationship, it simply forges a new type of relationship—one based not on physical presence but on memory, spirit, and love.

There are many wonderful books available that address acute grief and how to cope with it. But these books often focus on crisis management and imply that there is an "end" to mourning. They essentially fail to address the issue of grief's ongoing impact, and how it changes through the years. This book will focus on long-term adaptation to loss. It will provide you with the understanding of how loss can be integrated into your life, how it will continue to be a part of your existence through the years. This book will also give you the tools to take the loss and make it meaningful, that is, to find ways to ensure that your loved one's life and death were not in vain.

In part 1 of this book we will look at three basic stages of acute grief—Shock, Disorganization, and Reconstruction—which normally take place in the first year or two of bereavement. In part 2 we will look beyond acute grief to the rest of your life and what you should expect from your grief through the years. One chapter examines the fluid, lifelong process I call Synthesis, that of integrating life with loss. This stage is not optional, because as long as you are a breathing, feeling, loving person, you will forever be integrating loss into your life. Your grief will undoubtedly change over time, but it will never be "finished." The next chapter describes Transcendence, the fluid, lifelong process of making meaning out of loss. Trancendence *is* optional, since not everyone chooses to convert their pain into something meaningful.

In fact, in my personal and professional experience, I have seen grievers take one of two metaphorical roads over time. One road is dark and treacherous. Those on this path have let their loss dampen their spirits and, ultimately, extinguish the light from their lives. The other road is light and glimmering. Grievers on this path have learned from their grief, have been transformed by it, and have channeled it back into living. I am reminded of the Chinese symbol for crisis: one of the translations of this symbol is "danger," but, interestingly, another translation is "opportunity." Crisis, then, means both danger *and* opportunity. Grief over time is like that—it also offers both danger and opportunity.

This means that while grief is painful, it can lead to something positive; it has a transcendent potential. I have found an analogy helpful in illustrating this concept. If you're scheduled to depart on an airplane during a grey, drizzling day, you know that you will ascend through the rain and the dark clouds—usually after quite some delay, however—and you will rise through the storm to find bright sunshine up above. You transcend the darkness to find light. Transcendence literally means "rising above." With grief, over time, it is possible to rise above the stormy clouds to discover sunshine up above. But even as the sun shines brightly overhead, the tempest still blusters below.

Why is it that some grievers stay soaked in the rain? Why is it that they see only the "danger" as they live out their years feeling afraid, cold, and bitter? And why is it that others find the "opportunity" in crisis, using their grief as a catalyst for growth and maturity, and thus transcend toward the sun? Why are these people able to continue to risk and love, and even to believe in God, in spite of their broken hearts? And perhaps more importantly, how can *you* be one of those who discovers the transformative potential of grief?

To try to answer some of these questions, I began my research by talking to grievers whose losses occurred, on average, five or more years ago. I wanted to see what kind of perspective they had developed over time. I wanted to analyze grief's ongoing impact on their lives. And I wanted to see if there were trends and specific pathways leading toward transcendence.

Finding people who had lost and grieved was surprisingly easy. I told friends, colleagues, acquaintances—virtually anyone who would listen—about my project. I hoped to talk with people who had lost a spouse or partner, a child, a parent, and/or a sibling two or more years previously and would be willing to tell me about their experiences. One interview led to another. Friends of friends led me to more. It seemed that almost everybody knew someone who was a likely interview candidate. I was reminded of an old story about a woman who was promised eternal riches if she could find a house that had never known sorrow. She spent years traveling through many lands, going from house to house, and finally concluded that no such home exists. Indeed, every home knows sorrow.

I spoke with approximately fifty people, who represent all walks of life: men and women from all cultures and races, from all socioeconomic backgrounds, from all over the country. Their losses cover a wide spectrum and occurred anywhere from two to forty years ago. I have changed most of their names and identifying characteristics, but their experiences are true and the words are their own. Their stories are woven throughout this book.

What I learned from my conversations with these grievers is the basis for this book. I discovered that there is a way to grieve effectively and a way for grief to provide fuel for living. Those who see opportunity in crisis, who look toward the open rather than the closed doors, have certain qualities and characteristics in common. This mix of similar qualities seems critical for long-term healing, and I have framed it within a four-letter acronym called *SOAR*: Spirituality, Outreach, Attitude, and Reinvestment. Healthy grievers follow some or all of these pathways in order to move through the stages of grief and to reach the ultimate stage of healing that I have called Transcendence.

Transcendence has to do with rising above your immediate circumstances, achieving a new perspective, and in so doing, discovering possibilities for a future. When you're in the midst of pain, the future may seem incomprehensible. But Transcendence shows us that it is possible to have a vision for the future, a future filled with meaning *in addition to the loss*. The SOAR framework makes the vision a dynamic reality.

Part 3 of this book is devoted to explaining the SOAR Solution. This section seeks to guide you on your quest to find the numerous opportunities in grief, rather than only the never-ending, frozen sorrow. Although the road is not an easy one, this book offers a specific map for the journey. Each of the four chapters describing the four pathways of SOAR includes many real-life examples of how people have journeyed toward Transcendence in coping with their grief through the years. Bear in mind that SOAR is not a quick fix or a formula answer, since each person's journey down each pathway is complex and unique, but I hope that this framework will provide you with hope, guidance, and inspiration for making your own journey through danger and opportunity.

Of course, as I have already pointed out, not everyone reaches Transcendence—it's a *potential* stage of growth. Many people get stuck in the grieving process and are paralyzed by the spiritual and emotional roadblocks they encounter on the journey. In part 4 of this book, then, we will analyze these multiple blocks. One typical obstruction is a spiritual and religious crisis of faith. While this is not unusual in itself—in fact, it is characteristic of grief—if grievers cannot work through the crisis of faith and ultimately reconstruct a viable belief system, then they remain transfixed in a spiritual void. An entire chapter explores this frequently experienced phenomenon.

In another chapter we will look at the various types of emotional blocks, such as exaggerated grief, in which a perpetual griever wears his pain as a heavy cloak and thus is unable to move forward in life or to risk loving again. We also will consider the nongrieving or repressed griever, someone who constructs elaborate defenses to avoid feeling the pain, anger, guilt, hurt. I often see this type of patient in my practice, one who seeks help for another seemingly unrelated symptom, such as depression, anxiety, or substance abuse, only to discover that she is reacting to an unresolved loss from the past. If the emotional pain from loss isn't appropriately grieved, then the pain simply redirects itself into other destructive tendencies and behaviors.

Fortunately, it is never too late to do the grief work and it's never too late to transcend. Part 5 offers specifics on how to get back on track in a way that facilitates healing. You cannot rewrite history; the death of your loved one is a reality. But you do have a choice now in how you consciously respond to your grief and in how you weave its thread into the tapestry of your life. It is never too late to seek higher ground in your grief, to choose the SOAR pathways that lead toward Transcendence.

Considering the emotionally charged nature of this topic, I wasn't sure how working on this project would affect me personally. In fact, when I told people I was writing a book on death and grief, they would say, "Oh, how depressing" or "What a terrible topic." This underscored my impression that most people are terrified of this subject matter. Certainly, some of the interviews were quite painful for me, as the listener. Many were dreadfully sad. All were intense and emotional. I might have ended up depressed by the entire experience and obsessed with loss. Instead, what I gained by talking with each person is what I hope you will gain: a profound respect for the triumph of the human spirit and an increased awareness of life as a gift. As Rabbi Harold Kushner, who wrote *When Bad Things Happen to Good People,* said when I interviewed him regarding the death of his son, "The death of somebody you love is so painful and tragic precisely because life is so precious. By hurting so deeply, you are affirming the value of life."

This is a book about death and grief, yes, but more important, it's a book about love and hope. I have learned from my experience and interviews with courageous people about pain, struggle, resiliency, and meaning. Their stories show that over time, you can learn to transcend even in spite of the pain. We all get broken by life sooner or later because loss is the price we pay for living and loving. But experience shows that we can become stronger at the broken places and find the opportunity in crisis. I hope this book will help you move beyond grief and will guide you on your journey through times of healing and transcendence.

PART I

———

The Initial Grief Journey

CHAPTER 1

In the Beginning: Shock

If we could read the secret history of our
enemies, we should find in each man's
life sorrow and suffering enough to
disarm all hostility.
—HENRY WADSWORTH LONGFELLOW

Your journey along the grief road actually began long, long ago, with your very first breath of life. When you were born, you descended the birth canal, reluctantly leaving behind a warm and safe environment, finding yourself thrust into a cold, bright world, and possibly even getting whacked on the feet or the behind. That's when you had your first experience with loss. No wonder you cried! Every day thereafter you have experienced thousands of minor and major losses— from the loss of the bottle to the loss of a job, from the loss of your baby teeth to the loss of a friendship, from the loss of childhood innocence to the loss of adult dreams.

Every life transition, every beginning and ending you've ever experienced, involved loss. That includes even "happy" transitions—like graduation, marriage, the birth of a baby, a move to a new city, or a new job. Perhaps you don't expect to "grieve" when you have a baby, since it is such a joyous occasion, but with this event comes an important ending—the end of your life as a twosome, the end of a certain lifestyle that included freedom and spontaneity, the end of ever sleeping late again on a Saturday morning. Every parent will tell you that having a baby involves an "adjustment" period as they adapt to their new situation. Effectively they are grieving. Life is full of painful endings not related specifically to death, such as a job loss, an illness, a romantic breakup or divorce, and each of these also requires a transition stage as the old is discarded and the new is formulated.

So the truth is that, whether you realize it or not, you've actually been grieving on some level throughout your life. Clearly some losses are more traumatic than others, and some are harder to adapt to, thus requiring more time and energy. In fact, your loss now may bring the most intense grief that you've ever encountered, since death is the most extreme and dramatic of all losses. But it's not the first loss you've adapted to, and it's not, undoubtedly, the last. That's why understanding the grieving process is critical, since it is a relentless reality approaching each of us at every turn in life.

A Process

I once had a patient in therapy who used to wish for a magic button to push or a switch to flick that would make all of her troubles disappear. Whenever we reached a particularly emotional or painful part of her treatment, she would half-jokingly say, "Now where is that switch for me to flick to make this go away?" I think we've all wished for such a switch, at one time or another. You probably want one now more than ever. But unfortunately, no such magic button exists no matter how hard we might wish it.

Grieving is a process. As this book will consistently reinforce, grieving is a *lifelong* process. And yet, the first year of bereavement is particularly acute, as the effects of the loss begin to sink in, as each important holiday, anniversary, and birthday passes without the loved one's presence. Confronting the first anniversary of the death day is also a major psychological challenge. An old adage asserts that true healing cannot begin until the griever passes through each of the four seasons without his or her loved one.

So what happens in the first year and how do you cope with it? The grieving process is different for each, yet intrinsically the same for all, falling into three primary phases: stage one, Shock, characterized by numbness and disbelief; stage two, Disorganization, involving a physical, psychological, and often spiritual breakdown; and stage three, Reconstruction, or rebuilding one's life. "Stage" is an artificial concept in the sense that you don't progress linearly from one stage to the next, easily closing the door behind you. Most people tend to flow back and forth between stages two and three, at first spending more time in stage two, and eventually more in stage three.

Essentially grief is a tearing down and then building back up—a death and a resurrection. The death of a loved one irrevocably alters your life; in effect, it destroys your life as you knew it. Hopefully, through the grieving process, you begin to rebuild your life. What often happens, however, is that people want to avoid the painful aspects of stage two; the breakdown is too terrifying. So they rush right ahead to the stage of Reconstruction, telling others—and themselves—

that "Everything's just fine, I'm okay, I'm adjusting just fine." They attempt to skip to the end before they've gone through the middle.

A friend recently told me about her neighbor whose four-year-old-son, an only child, died tragically, unexpectedly, suddenly. My friend, who also has a four-year-old-child, said, "You wouldn't believe how well she is handling it. I saw her last week, just a few months after his death, and she seemed just fine, so composed. I got all choked up, started crying when I saw her—I could hardly speak, but she was like a pillar of strength. She said they were going to try to have another baby. I was so impressed by her ability to move on."

What I said to my friend was, "It sounds to me like she's 'moving on' just a little too quickly. I just hope she's allowing herself to break down in private. Or if she can't touch the pain yet, I hope she'll let herself get there eventually. That's the only way she'll ever truly heal." What I thought to myself was, "It's amazing that people really think stoicism is admirable." Unfortunately, stoicism is the antithesis of true healing. People need to understand that and not be so afraid of consciously experiencing the pain.

Imagine the consequences of leaping to the end before you've gone through the middle if you had a broken leg from an accident. Imagine that you're lying in bed in a cast just one week after the accident. Would you try to take the cast off by yourself and go out dancing that night? Of course not. You would understand that your bones needed time to heal, time to knit back together in an orderly, chronological progression. The process cannot be rushed. Well, grieving follows the same pattern. Your mind, heart, and spirit need time to heal, and the process cannot be rushed.

Sure, you can go dancing on your broken grief without giving it time to heal, without taking your medicine or doing your physical therapy. You might even find yourself dancing rather well at first. But look deeply and take care because your breath may be short, you may start to trip, and your dancing shoes may be deteriorating. There are no real shortcuts or switches to flick.

Wherever you are right now on your journey—whether your loved one died two weeks ago, two years ago, or even twenty years ago, it helps to understand the process from beginning to the not-so-clear end. As Glenda the Good Witch of the North told Dorothy in *The Wizard of Oz* before she set out for Emerald City, "It's always best to start at the beginning." So it is with most things; so it is with grief.

Shock

The first wave of shock occurs the moment you discover that your loved one is dead, or is going to die. A feeling of numbness sets in and you might feel as if you are in a dream. Disbelief is common since the mind simply cannot absorb such overwhelming news. You might think, "This can't be happening; she's not really dead; this is just a bad dream and any minute now I'll wake up." Some people faint or find that they feel dizzy or even nauseated. Anything is possible in this stage: you may cry hysterically or you may be unable to shed a tear; you may make all of the funeral arrangements or be unable to function.

Shock at this time is actually a protective mechanism, an emotional anesthesia that eases the pain. Your mind, like your body, can only absorb a finite amount of trauma at any given time. Just as a body goes into shock after physical impact, so does your mind. The sense of numbness and denial is highly adaptive since it allows the reality of the tragedy to sink in slowly and gives you time to mobilize your inner resources. The shock response usually lasts anywhere from a few hours to a few weeks.

Suse is a fifty-three-year-old woman who learned of her son's death by telephone. Her son was murdered by terrorists in the fatal and very public bombing of Pan Am's flight 103, which exploded over Lockerbie, Scotland in December of 1988, killing all 270 people on board. Suse's son was one of the thirty-five Syracuse University students on the plane who had been spending a semester abroad and was en route home for the holidays. Suse, a professional sculptor, recalled:

I was so excited that Alexander was coming home that night for the holidays, and I just couldn't wait to see him. We had a big family vacation planned, and I was filled with anticipation. That afternoon, I was working in my studio, on a figure of Alexander, in fact. The phone rang and it was a young friend of Alexander's and she asked me in a peculiar tone of voice, only because it was so slow, if Alexander was home yet. I said, "No, but why don't you leave a message, he'll be home tonight." She said, "No, that's all right. What time do you expect him home?" And I said what time. And she said, "What airline is he coming home on?" And I said, "It's Pan Am." And she said, "Do you know the number?" And I said, "Yes, Pan Am 103." And she just blurted out, "Oh my God, haven't you heard? It exploded." I remember how something in my gut just tightened. It was like something was completely sucked out of me, all my life, all my innards, and I screamed at her not to say such a thing. But I knew that this was not a joke. I hung up. I bent over, clutching my stomach, and I went over to the radio. The first thing I heard was, "Pan Am 103 was last seen in a fireball over Scotland." That was the moment I knew that I would never see him again. I fell to the ground and I thought I was going to faint.

Although it has been many years since this tragic event, Suse cried bitterly as she told me this story. The emotion welled up inside her as she recounted that terrible moment in time when her world changed forever. Words are inadequate to express the horror of learning that someone you love has been wrenched from your life.

With sudden death, one minute your loved one is with you, loving you, laughing with you, arguing with you, and then suddenly he vanishes as if by some cruel magic trick. There's no time to say goodbye, to adjust to the idea gradually. The electrifying jolt makes life seem as fragile and ephemeral as a child's bubble that bursts moments after being blown through a plastic ring. Understandably, with a sudden death, shock may be especially intense and possibly prolonged.

After the initial brutal impact, shock generally continues with a wave of aftershocks. These aftershocks can leave you in a daze lasting for weeks or even months. In this fog, you know on one level that your loved one has died, but on another level you cannot grasp all of the ramifications. It seems impossible to fathom that the person you love, who was just alive, is suddenly no longer there. Life may seem dreamlike, surreal. Suse said, "Initially you're not sane. You don't think and you don't function. Waking up was the worst. Waking up in the morning was just a major, major ordeal."

During these aftershocks, it's not uncommon to "forget" that your loved one is gone. You might set a place for him at the dinner table only to later dissolve into tears as you realize that no one will be sitting there. You might reach for her on the other side of the bed in the middle of the night only to rediscover that you are alone. Maybe you pick up the phone and dial your brother's number before you realize that no, he's not there to answer. It's not unusual, in this stage, to repeatedly do or think something related to your loved one as if he were still alive. Over and over again you come up against the cold, hard, shocking truth that he is really gone, forever.

Shock will be influenced by whether death came like a blow from behind with no preparation and no warning, as in Suse's case, or if it came slowly, gingerly and lingered for months or even years. If your loved one is dying from a terminal illness, for example, there is a certain amount of anticipatory grieving that you can do, since you have a sense of preparation for the death.

Anticipated death may in fact seem welcome by comparison, at least to someone who has had the wind swiftly knocked out of him by sudden death. But the truth is that anticipated death has its own brand of shock, a dissipated impact that may be reexperienced over time. With a terminal illness, for example, you experience shock in the beginning with the diagnosis. You also experience the shock of watching your loved one deteriorate, and then you may experience shock anew with the actual death, after you were somehow secretly hoping for a cure.

Andrew's lover, John, was diagnosed with AIDS shortly after they began their relationship.

I knew he was HIV positive, but this was 1988 and everything was relatively new; it was still in the researching stage. He would joke about having two or less years to live but I figured something would happen in that time, some medical advance that would save him. Soon, I realized how sick he was and he said I could leave if I wanted. But how could I? I had found that special person. No way. I wouldn't have left. I spent an entire year doing nothing but taking care of him. He became blind and deaf, literally helpless; tubes were everywhere. Watching him deteriorate was the hardest part. He went from the person I knew and loved, to this shell of himself.

Because John's death was expected, Andrew had an opportunity to say goodbye. There was time to take care of unfinished business, time to plan for the end. But time worked against Andrew as well because time meant becoming a caretaker and watching the person he loved change, ravaged by illness. Although theoretically Andrew wasn't caught off guard by John's death, he still experienced shock repeatedly as he mourned the past, the present, and the future. In some ways, even with advanced warning, you can never be prepared for death.

I think at one point John shut down and just waited for the end to come. When he died, I couldn't even cry. I was in shock; numb, absolutely numb. Even though I knew it was coming, this wasn't supposed to happen. He was only twenty-eight and I'm forty—I was supposed to die first. I've known other people who have died, but this affected me more than anything I could ever imagine. It turned my whole life around when he died. I just kept thinking, "This isn't the way it's supposed to be. My life isn't supposed to be like this now."

It's not uncommon to experience relief after the lingering death of someone you loved. On the one hand you're relieved for your loved one who no longer suffers. You're glad that the process of pain and deterioration has ended at last. On the other hand, you're relieved for yourself since your life no longer has to be put on hold. Many caretakers find that their lives revolved around the illness, and that they sacrificed everything—time, money, energy—for months or even years. To finally be released from this responsibility may understandably bring about some sense of relief.

Of course, with relief may come guilt as you may be ashamed of thinking, "At last it's finally over and I can move on with my life." You think there's something wrong with feeling a sense of personal gain from someone else's death. Working through the feelings will take time, but eventually you need to come to a place of acceptance. You deserve to get on with your life and the best thing you can do for yourself is give yourself permission to live and realize that feeling relief is normal.

Coping

During this time of shock, you must remember that you are in a highly vulnerable state, both physically and emotionally. You need to be extremely gentle with yourself and not expect too much. It may be all you can do to take a shower on any given day. Don't push yourself. If possible, have people around who can answer the phone for you and cook your meals. Also, if possible, take some time off from work. Most companies will offer several condolence days and some will even agree to several weeks off. This is really a time to focus on your survival, just one day at a time.

Many people find it helpful initially to be surrounded by loved ones, friends and family who can offer support. First of all, they can take care of any details for you that you don't think you can manage on your own. Second, something healing occurs when you connect to other people. A traditional Native American expression reflects the wisdom of being with family and friends: "Joy shared is doubled and grief shared is halved." They can connect you to your lost love by sharing their memories with you. And they can hug you, touch you, hold you. Physical touch is extremely therapeutic, especially when you are grieving. So literally find a shoulder to cry on.

On the other hand, some people prefer to be alone in the beginning of their grief. One griever told me that she couldn't stand all the visitors and well-wishers around after her husband died. She said, "I know that their intentions were good, but I just didn't really want to be around anyone yet. And I especially didn't feel comfortable crying in front of everybody. At one point, there were so many people in my living room that I just got up and took a shower so that I could cry there in peace. I just sobbed in the shower. Everyone kept telling me that I shouldn't be left alone, but that's really all I wanted in the beginning."

Every individual has different needs and preferences. The most important thing is to respect the shock and experience it in whatever way you instinctively need to. Whatever feels right to you—whether it's to cry hysterically, or to be alone and stare at the wall, or to be surrounded by friends—then do it.

Facing the Grief

Each stage has certain conditions, or goals, associated with it. Successfully achieving them lets you know that your grieving is proceeding in an appropriate manner. You must meet these goals not just once; you must meet and remeet them, over and over again. The goal for the stage of Shock is to accept the reality that your loved one is dead. In other words, the denial that is so adaptive in this stage must be dissolved. By the end of this stage, you must have moved beyond any hope, any confusion, any lingering fantasies that your loved one is still alive or will somehow return. You must know and admit deep down in your soul that your beloved is truly, irrevocably gone from this planet, at least in the physical sense. This doesn't mean that you have to like the reality of the loss, only that you acknowledge its truth.

One concrete way to help accomplish this goal is to attend the funeral. A friend of mine once said that when she dies, she doesn't want to have a funeral because she doesn't want all of her family to sit around and cry for her. She thinks funerals are morbid. Nothing could be further from the truth. First of all, her family will be sad no matter what, even without a funeral. But without it, they will be deprived of an important mourning ritual. The funeral or memorial service is one of the most tangible ways to share your grief with others and it is a vital, socially sanctioned ritual for acknowledging your loss.

The funeral or memorial service is a specific activity that can help you resolve your shock and achieve the goal of accepting the reality of the loss. I discourage grievers from taking any sedatives during the funeral. Even though you may think you need medication to "get through it," doing so will prevent you from experiencing a very important ceremony. Although you may sit through the funeral in somewhat of a natural daze, it is still preferable to a medicated daze, because on some level the message will sink in that your loved one, your precious one, is gone.

At the burial site, after his lover died of AIDS, Andrew finally began to absorb the reality of what was happening. "His funeral was arranged quickly, but I didn't even cry at the funeral. I just sat there, numb. Truly it didn't hit me until we took the body to the cemetery. When the casket was lowered into the ground, I just lost it. It wasn't over until then."

A funeral or memorial service also celebrates the life of your loved one. You honor the deceased, play his favorite music, or read passages from a favorite book. You review his life and how he affected this world. This special service is a tribute to the one who touched your life so deeply and it is a beautiful way to show respect for his life. Furthermore, it celebrates the relationship that you had and commemorates the special love that you shared.

Of course, sometimes there are circumstances that absolutely preclude your being at the funeral. Maybe it's geographically too far, financially prohibitive, or you have an unavoidable conflict. In this situation, I would recommend devising your own private ritual to commemorate the death. Either gather a few people who knew your loved one, or if you prefer, conduct the ritual alone. You might review some pictures of your loved one, light a candle, choose some comforting music. Read some inspirational literature and say a prayer. The entire event may take only ten minutes but the therapeutic value is immeasurable. Our culture, unlike many others, has few rituals to demarcate life's important passages. But we always have the option of creating our own.

Be Gentle

The point is that getting through these first few weeks will not be easy and you need to rally as many supportive, comforting, consoling things around you as you can. Whether death came suddenly, expectedly, or somewhere in between, you need to be gentle with yourself in your shock. It's a temporal stage that cannot be rushed or forced. It lasts as long as necessary until your mind begins to absorb the magnitude of what has happened. Reality will come crashing in only too soon as you accept the fact that your loved one is gone. You will emerge slowly from the fog, finding yourself sinking in the quicksand of grief as you move into the stage of Disorganization.

CHAPTER 2

The Heart of Grief: Disorganization

The great object of life is sensation—to feel
that we exist, even in pain.
—LORD BYRON

After the stage of Shock, grievers commonly enter the stage of Disorganization. This is the heart of grief, and thus the most difficult. Now the whole gamut of feelings comes pouring forth: pain, anger, depression, guilt, sadness, anxiety, fear, loneliness, relief. You will most likely feel flooded by the feelings, overwhelmed, as they wash over you in unbearable crashing waves. You know that your life will never be the same.

You remember the good times and the precious, ordinary moments. You remember the bad times and all the things you wish you had said that you'll never be able to say now. Some days are punctuated by gut-wrenching, bittersweet, lonely moments, but on other days, you don't feel anything at all. You might have nightmares, health problems, or irrational phobias. You probably think that you're going crazy and you may even want to die. This is a particularly difficult stage since it seems endless and in fact it may reemerge, off and on, for many years.

Grievers say things to me like, "Is it right to be angry at my husband for leaving me?" or "I'm in so much pain that I can't sleep or eat," or "Do you think I'm going crazy?" These responses are perfectly normal. You may think you are losing your mind, but you are not. The intense, raw feelings that you have are all part of the natural, healthy grieving process.

For many, the first year of grief is extremely difficult because the loss is still so fresh, so recent. You must go through an entire year's cycle of events—birthdays, anniversaries, holidays—each for the first time without your beloved. You must face each dreaded event as it dredges up feeling after feeling. In the first year you are confronted with all of the secondary losses as well, all those big and small losses that come in addition to the death of your loved one. You discover that your wife knew how to organize your finances and now you haven't a clue what to do. Or your son always took care of the pets and now you don't even know what kind of food they eat. Waves of loss hit you at every turn and you are flooded by feelings with an unprecedented rawness.

For others in the first year of bereavement, life continues on automatic pilot and most things are business as usual. It is only later, sometimes years later, that the feelings emerge in their full fury. It is not unusual for pain to surface many years after the fact.

Your grief journey will be unique just as you are unique. Your grief will be influenced by a mixture of personal, circumstantial, and cultural forces. Things like your age, your gender, your relationship with the deceased, your personality, your previous experiences with loss, your belief systems, how your loved one died—all of these variables will interact with how you process your grief.

If your husband died suddenly in a car accident, you will have different issues to contend with than if you're a mother whose child dies of cancer. If you are a Buddhist you will handle grief differently than if you are a Christian. As a widow, your challenges will be affected by your age, since a thirty-year-old widow has different challenges than a seventy-year-old widow. Maybe this is the first major death in your family and you have virtually no frames of reference. On the other hand, maybe you've lost so many people that one more seems unendurable.

But even as your journey is individual, there are certain universal experiences and feelings among grievers. The first part of this chapter will describe many of the feelings that you *might* have in this stage of Disorganization. You may feel all of them, or only a few. Knowing about some of the conflicting, overlapping feelings that others have encountered along the grief road may be helpful to you on your own journey. One of my patients told me, "I had no idea what to do because this was the page in the instruction book of life that I hadn't gotten. I wasn't prepared for this and I had no idea what was to come." It helps to know what might be coming.

Grief is not an illness. The feelings described in the next several pages are the mind, body, and spirit's natural reaction to being robbed, to having one's heart ripped apart and one's world blown wide open. Therefore, grief cannot be "cured." It must be worked through, adapted to, and incorporated into your life. Later in this chapter we will focus on the grief work—facing and experiencing the feelings—for that is the healing goal for the second stage. Although processing these feelings is extremely difficult, it is the only road for true healing. We will explore specific strategies for absorbing and expressing the feelings in this very painful and intense stage of grief.

ANGER

Anger is often a predominant initial feeling that overshadows everything, especially in the beginning. It might feel like an amorphous sensation that just oozes out of you and is directed at anything and everything that comes into your path. Or you may channel your anger toward a specific person, such as the deceased, for leaving you alone and abandoning you: "How could you leave me now? How dare you?" Many people feel guilty for being angry at the dead, but it's extremely common.

You might also be angry at God. Or perhaps it's the doctor who infuriated you, who couldn't save your loved one. Or was it another person responsible for the death? Or the criminal justice system that's unfair? When something terrible happens and you're in pain, a natural reaction is to lash out and blame someone. It helps restore order if you can pin the blame or at least channel the anger into something that makes sense.

As you might imagine, Suse, whose son was killed on Pan Am 103, was plagued with anger about her son's death. It was a very complicated death, involving an airline, terrorists, the State Department, our government, foreign governments. Clearly, there were ample directions that Suse could aim her anger.

As time went by and we started to function a little bit more normally, it occurred to us, "Oh my God, what happened here?" But as with all things in life, I try to be balanced, which is one of the hardest things to do, really. At times, my anger gets the upper hand. I see those young faces and I think what had they ever done to deserve the luck that they got? Plus the fact that our lives will never be as they were. We were innocent and now we're not innocent anymore. That's a terrific reason to be angry. Plus the fact that Alexander only got twenty-one years to live. He had hardly begun living. There are lots of reasons for anger.

I'm still sick at how he was shipped home. It was one of the ugliest things I could ever remember and it's unforgivable for a government like the United States to allow that to happen. We took it up with our State Department and we actually retrained the State Department so that this will never, ever happen again to another American citizen—being shipped home like garbage.

I have my good share of anger and hate, I really do. There are lots of reasons for anger. But I know that I cannot let that anger block me from the rest of my life. There's still a lot to do, a lot to live. I know that any one emotion out of whack and out of balance can block a life. But it's a constant battle.

Suse has a constant struggle on her hands but she has every right to be angry. Her son was an innocent victim in a game of terrorism. The bureaucracy afterward has been infuriating for all concerned. Before she can even hope to get through the anger and release it, she must thoroughly feel and express the rage.

You might also discover that you have an overwhelming sense of resentment, hatred even, toward those who haven't lost a loved one. As a young widow, you may look at the happy couples you know and feel rage and a gnawing sense of "Why are they happy and why did my husband die?" As a parent who lost his twenty-year-old son, you may look with bitterness, envy, and animosity at your friend whose son is graduating from college. You know on one level that your anger toward him is totally irrational, but you can't help yourself. One griever told me flat out, "Sometimes I wish other people's children were dead. Why should they be so happy? First I'm surprised by that feeling but then I say it's okay, it's perfectly normal to think and feel." Emotions aren't necessarily logical and clearly life is all too unfair.

For some, anger lasts for years and years. For others, it lasts only a few months. Anger is, in many ways, a "surface" emotion; it tends to mask a deeper feeling of pain and helplessness within. It's easier to be angry than sad. That's why for many, holding onto anger can last so long, because it's often easier than going the next level deeper, to pain. Anger can also be directed within, which often results in an overwhelming sense of guilt.

GUILT

You might feel guilty that you didn't resolve things while you had the chance. If only you had said, "I'm sorry." Or if only you had asked for forgiveness. You blame yourself. You tell yourself that you didn't do enough for your loved one. You didn't call enough; you never thanked him for everything; you shouldn't have insisted that he go to the store;

you're sorry you said something hurtful to him; you wish you had said "I love you." You feel guilty for the things you did, but you also feel guilty for the things you didn't do. Your guilt takes you around and around irrationally, unproductively.

Guilt is especially common with suicides. Suicide is a death like no other because it means your loved one intentionally chose to die. Chances are high that you feel somehow responsible for the death, as if you could have or should have been able to prevent it. You might think, "Why didn't I see this coming and stop it?" You look back on the warning signals, the hints left, and punish yourself for either not taking them seriously or not trying hard enough to help. You blame yourself unmercifully.

Society's reaction isn't much help either since there is still some shame and stigma attached to suicide. You might feel the target of a silent accusation: "Why was he so unhappy in his life that he chose to die?" "What's wrong with your family?" "Did you drive him to it?" Perhaps you lie about the cause of death and tell people a story other than the truth. Only AIDS has this similar mixture of grief with disgrace, death with dishonor.

Sylvia, a fifty-six-year-old woman, lost her twenty-six-year-old son to suicide ten years ago. Her son, Bill, was a deeply troubled young man. He grew up with an abusive, violent, alcoholic father who told him when he was a child, "I should have thrown you down the toilet bowl when you were born." When Bill was fifteen he used to say, "I wish I was dead," and at eighteen he made his first suicide attempt. At the age of twenty-five, he was unemployed and living at home. After much conflict, several arguments, and a lot of tears, Sylvia reluctantly asked Bill to leave her home because she believed that he needed to be out on his own and that she was becoming a crutch for him. He moved to Florida and began building a life for himself, including finding a girlfriend and a job with the city government. Unfortunately, he was soon laid off from his job due to budget cuts and spiraled into a deep depression. He began drinking and said he was afraid of becoming violent, like his father. Sylvia, concerned, went down to visit him.

I begged him to come home with me to Brooklyn. I knew he was in trouble. He wouldn't have even been there if I hadn't pushed him out of the house, and to this day, I feel guilty for doing it. He wouldn't listen to me and he told me to leave him alone. When I was on the plane home, I felt like something had happened. It turns out he shot himself in the head while I was on the plane. For six months I was depressed and numb. I would go into the grocery store and think "What am I doing here? How can I go shopping when this terrible thing happened? How can normal things go on when I just buried my son?" I couldn't help my boy. I felt I had turned my back on him. I actually got on a plane and left him. I kept searching and searching as to why this happened. I thought I was going crazy.

Sylvia feels guilty because she worries that she in some way contributed to her son's sense of despair and desperation. She couldn't save her boy. It's important to note that this was her *son* who committed suicide, not her father or her sister. Some people feel that the death of a child, no matter what the child's age, is the most unspeakable, the most profoundly painful of all losses. A child is the person you gave life to and nurtured, a part of yourself. When a child dies, so does the future. You expect your children to outlive you, to be your immortality. When Sylvia feels guilty, part of her guilt is the kind of irrational guilt that many parents feel for not being "good enough," not being able to take care of and protect their child from all of life's pains.

However, Sylvia didn't kill her son, she didn't end his life. She was not responsible for her son's death. He was the one who chose to die. His actions were made under duress, with his judgment impaired by a debilitating depression. Guilt has a brutal stronghold, but most guilt is not accurate or truly warranted. Learning to let go and forgive yourself is a vital part of the healing process.

Ultimately guilt needs to be experienced before it can be released. Guilt enslaves and paralyzes initially, but that is normal. You will soon come to accept that you cannot rewrite the script of what has already occurred. Just as with the other feelings, it will require time and care to embrace the guilt, work through it, and use it to mobilize yourself toward new growth and forgiveness.

PAIN

Beneath the anger, beneath the guilt, lies a primal pain. Grief *is* painful; there's just no way around it. It feels dull and aching one minute and searing and stabbing the next. Pain may shoot through your body sharply like a physical injury or just gnaw slowly away at your mind. It burns with anguish, leaves you trembling from the racking despair. Many grievers describe feeling as if part of their heart has been torn apart. Others refer to a painful void in their bodies, as if there is an empty, bomb-ravaged cavity within. The obvious truth is that grief hurts.

Emily Dickinson put it well:

Pain has an element of blank;
It cannot recollect
When it began, or if there were
A day when it was not.

It has no future but itself,
Its infinite realms contain
Its past, enlightened to perceive
New periods of pain.

Indeed, when you're in the midst of pain, it is all-encompassing and you find it difficult to recall "a day when it was not." Emotional pain resembles physical pain in that sense. For example, if you're hanging a picture on a wall, and you accidentally hammer your thumb instead of the nail, your finger throbs and aches so that it takes your breath away. All of a sudden, your thumb seems bigger than the rest of your body. Perhaps it is even sore for several days. You cannot imagine a time when your thumb *didn't* hurt so much . . . and you never truly appreciated how incredibly valuable your thumb was until now. Emotional pain similarly overshadows everything and threatens to swallow you up whole.

Jamie is a twenty-nine-year-old woman whose father died of a massive heart attack when she was a sophomore in college.

I was just done with exams and my sister and brother-in-law were coming on Friday to pick me up. I was so excited because the next semester I was going away to Israel. But when they came to get me, I could tell something was wrong. My sister started crying and she said, "It's Daddy." I began hysterically crying and screaming. I was very much Daddy's little girl—I adored my father. His death was devastating for all of us; it was so unexpected. I never had an opportunity to say goodbye and I love you. I was so shattered, but my mother told me I had to be strong for other people.

For a long time, I felt deadened inside. I tried to keep a normal life going, but I couldn't even sit on his side of the bed when I went home to visit. A part of me died with him. I can only explain it as being ripped in half—the two parents who make you and form you and then suddenly one is gone. It feels like a devastating void. A teacher once told me no matter how old you get, you're never truly an adult until you've buried a parent. The severing of the child/parent bond is unlike any other. I think that's very true.

Most college students expect to study hard and play hard, but they don't expect to grapple with grief. Jamie was hit with a loss that was unexpected and devastating. When she returned to college, no one knew how to respond to her. They had never encountered such a loss and had no idea what to say or do. Most people said nothing. The rest of her college years, the rest of her life, has been informed by this loss. "I didn't end up going to Israel that junior year. I was too distraught, and I really couldn't move on with my life for a long time. Eventually I did move on, but it still hurts

. . . even today. I felt the loss at not having him at my wedding, all the significant events in my life. I go on, but I miss him. I wonder what life would have been like if he were here now."

As we age, eventually we do expect to outlive our parents, at least consciously. Such a loss is considered "normal," since it's in keeping with our expected life cycle. Unfortunately that doesn't make it any less painful, for although we expect it, we can never be prepared. As one griever said, "On some basic, primal level, you never really expect your *mommy* to die." So when she does, it hurts the child as well as the adult in you.

A parent, to your unconscious, is the omnipotent being who will take care of you, guide you, and make everything okay. Your parent gave you life, nurtured you, and loved you. And if she didn't successfully accomplish this, to your unconscious, your parent is the omnipotent being who *should* have done all those things. A part of you perhaps always had the unconscious fantasy that your parent would change. Once she dies, you lose the reality and the fantasy. You must detach from the lost dream as well as from the lost person.

DEPRESSION

Once you begin to let in some of the pain, chances are you'll react to it with either depression or anxiety. Many of the symptoms associated with psychiatric clinical depression are the exact symptoms you may experience: hopelessness, apathy, loneliness, lethargy, anxiety, appetite and sleep disturbance, sadness, loss of libido, inability to concentrate, difficulty getting out of bed. If you were not grieving and you experienced these symptoms consistently for more than two weeks, you would need to be evaluated for antidepressant medication. But if you are grieving and you experience these symptoms, then you are merely all too normal.

Laura, a tall and willowy thirty-three-year-old blond, knows the empty feeling that depression brings. She had been in an on-again, off-again relationship with a man for seven years. Their relationship had been tempestuous, but she always believed that she would spend the rest of her life with him. Five years ago, it looked as if they had finally worked everything out and they were planning a future together. That is, until the pickup truck he was in was hit by a drunk driver. His neck was broken and he was paralyzed from the neck down. He hung on in the hospital for two and a half weeks before finally dying.

I went to the hospital immediately. I had so much fear in those two weeks. Even though I wasn't legally married to him, I was married to him emotionally and mentally. There was always the desire and the expectation that we would be together. I was with him on the day that he died. I felt completely torn apart inside. The next few weeks and months were awful, just awful. I was twenty-six then and I went to my parents' house to live, from September to December. I don't even remember anything about that time. I felt so empty and shattered and black. It ripped out my insides. At the beginning, I didn't think I would survive.

Maybe the black hole was always there inside but his dying seared it open. I was angry at him for leaving me. Even today I'm still angry at him. For about three years, not a day went by where I wasn't thinking about him and feeling sad and lost—I mean really lost and depressed. I saw only black for ages; it took me a long time to see colors again.

For Laura, it took three years to work through her most intense feelings. But for the first several months after he died, from September to December, she fell apart. That was exactly what she needed to do. She retreated from the world; she licked her wounds. She stopped functioning. And although she didn't think that she would survive, she did.

ANXIETY

Another feeling that may come up is a pervasive sense of anxiety, dread, and nervousness. The first sentence of C. S. Lewis's beautiful book *A Grief Observed* is, "No one ever told me that grief felt so like fear." Yet when your world collapses and you see that the rug has been pulled out from under you, you are understandably lost. You feel powerless and therefore nervous. You may be plagued with irrational fears and even phobias. Perhaps you're afraid to go out in public lest you dissolve into tears. Feeling this way is completely normal. The world as you knew it no longer exists, and it will certainly take time to adjust to a new one.

After Steve's fiancée died of cancer, he began to experience anxiety attacks, complete with heart palpitations, dizziness, and sweaty palms. He said, "I felt acutely then, but still to this day, a sense of loss. Not just a loss that made me feel simply despondent, although it did that as well, but a sense of loss that made me feel tremendously alone and disconnected and almost scared—a sense of being helpless and feeling acted upon." Steve describes how he felt with the dawning realization that he couldn't control his world.

Many grievers describe feeling frightened, more aware of danger, more aware of loss. After Jamie's father died, she said, "I became hyper about illness. I guess I got panicked about life being taken away before its time. Sometimes I still get so frightened and fearful. Life seems so fragile and I wonder how I would cope if I lost my husband. When your ultimate fear is realized, you don't know how to put it inside and not be scared anymore."

Your fear may become so pervasive that you are terrified to be alone. Maybe you are terrified of crime, afraid of your own death, or petrified of becoming ill. Just know that fear, anxiety, terror are perfectly normal reactions to grief. As frightening as this feeling is, it's a natural reaction to having the foundation of your life crumble to dust.

LONELINESS

Loss of a partner is often considered one of the most devastating in terms of loneliness. Our society is geared toward finding that perfect person, Mr. or Ms. Right. We feel incomplete until we find our mate, and once we do, we expect to live happily ever after. Your spouse is someone you build your life with, day in and day out. Your lives are interdependent in hundreds of ways—you share finances, goals, values, possessions, a home, the raising of children, the daily struggles. You promise "to love, honor, and cherish, till death do us part," but you can never prepare for that moment.

When that person is gone, you are devastated. You might never have lived alone before. Some of your friends will dwindle away as they are uncomfortable being around a widow. Your social role, your entire identity has changed. Furthermore, research shows that the mortality rates for the recently widowed are higher than normal, and that the widowed tend to have more serious physical illnesses. This kind of grief can literally be deadly.

Novelist Gabriel García Márquez writes a poignant account of a woman sleeping in her bed just days after her husband's death, in *Love in the Time of Cholera*:

> She wept for the death of her husband, for her solitude and rage, and when she went into the empty bedroom she wept for herself. . . . Everything that belonged to her husband made her weep again: his tasseled slippers, his pajamas under the pillow. . . . Crushed by grief, she prayed to God to send her death that night while she slept. . . . She began to sob in her sleep, and she slept, sobbing, . . . until long after the roosters crowed and she was awakened by the despised sun of the morning without him.

García Márquez beautifully captures the pain and sadness that a griever feels when she loses the person with whom she had chosen to share her life. Andrew felt that kind of devastation after his lover, John, died from AIDS. They had lived together for four years.

> I was angry at John because he left me. He left me to be alone in that apartment. I had never spent a night there alone. I remember that night well. I went to bed and I opened the window. I heard every creak and sound. I did not sleep but finally began dozing at daybreak. I was so lonely. I walked from one room to the next all night thinking, "He's not here and he's not coming back." For the first year after he died, I worked

compulsively and would do anything to avoid being home alone. The bed was still so lonely and there was such a void in my life. The emptiness was pervasive.

Even if you didn't lose a spouse or partner, you can still be faced with loneliness. Maybe you lost your best friend. Maybe you lost someone who could always make you laugh or smile. You want more than anything to give that person a hug, to call her up on the phone and say hello, just to hear her voice. You *miss* your loved one more than anything on this earth. A world without her feels empty, desolate, lonely.

You might also feel lonely because, as a result of this death, you have lost a whole network of people in your life. For example, if you lose your only child, you lose him as well as your identity as a parent, your involvement at the school, your membership in the PTA, your participation in the car pool, and so on. You may feel uncomfortable around other parents, or vice versa, so you lose those friendships too. You lose important social connections and are filled with loneliness as a result. Not only have you lost your precious child, but you have lost an entire way of life.

Facing the Grief

Let's face it, there is a natural human terror of facing painful feelings. Who wouldn't want, on some level, to evade psychic trauma? Unconsciously, we believe that we cannot survive the feelings, that they will destroy us. One griever said, "I was afraid to feel, to cry, because I was afraid if I started I would just lose control and I might never stop." The myth is that the torrent of pain will wash us away.

Your temptation to escape may be so overwhelming that

you devise a number of ways to avoid the grief, to run from the reality. The most obvious way is to obliterate the feelings and deaden yourself by using drugs, alcohol, sex, food—anything to hide from the truth. Unfortunately, deadening yourself will not change the situation and will only serve to worsen things by creating an additional problem, substance abuse.

Another method of escape is to deny the impact of the emotion and act as if it doesn't exist. For each overwhelming feeling then, you devise a counteractive diffuser. Pain: It doesn't hurt that bad. Depression: Cheer Up! Anxiety: Calm down. Guilt: It's not your fault. Anger: Don't get mad. Or you might busy yourself with activities too soon or maybe tend to everyone else's pain rather than your own. You think, "I have to be strong for others," or "There's nothing I can do about it so I should just get back to business as usual." Possibly you minimize the grief or rationalize it away: "Oh, she was so old, it was time for her to die," or "At least he's out of his pain now—it was a blessing."

Each of these statements may, in fact, be true. But even if your loved one's death was a "blessing," you still need to address your loss. You still have wounds that need healing. You still must work through your grief, and unfortunately there are no short cuts. The only way out is through. Remember that the healing goal of this stage is to face and to experience the feelings. What does that mean? It means that no matter how terrifying and difficult it is, you must go straight through the heart of grief by identifying it, feeling it, absorbing it, and expressing it. In the rest of this chapter we will examine specific ways to do this.

TALKING

To begin with, you need to talk about the death. It sounds simplistic but the effect is nothing short of miraculous. First, you need to tell the story of the death—the details before, during, and after. In fact, you need to tell the story over and over and over again. After you've told it one hundred times, you need to tell it again. Retelling the story makes the death real to you and sweeps away any residue of denial. It starts the healing process of acceptance and exorcises the pain. When you talk, you give air to a raw wound that will otherwise fester. Think of talking as positive ventilation.

Second, you need to talk about your loved one. Tell people what he was like, what you loved about him, what you miss about him, favorite stories you have about him. This may seem masochistic at first, and will probably leave you crying every time, but you will derive strength in remembering the essence of your love. Also, you will begin the process of internalizing your beloved and you may find that talking about him makes you feel somehow closer.

Finally, you need to talk about your feelings about the death. Tell about how you miss your loved one, and what that specifically feels like. Talk out the feelings of pain, anger, guilt, or relief. Talk out your feelings of disbelief, despair, and hopelessness. You need to break out of your isolation and be heard. Talking out loud will help you identify what you are experiencing. And it will give your experience life. Having someone listen to you, witnessing your grief, actually validates your experience.

Ironically, many grievers don't have the opportunity to talk because no one asks them to. One griever told me about how she went back to work after her son died and no one asked her about her grief. People are afraid to broach this sensitive subject, afraid to stir up your pain, afraid to stir up their own pain. But the point is that the talking and the telling are therapeutic. The pain is there no matter what. Stirring it is the only way to live it and release it.

However, even once you find friends, colleagues, and family to talk with, after a while, they move on with their lives. You worry that you are burdening them with your troubles. They seem to tire of listening to you. People can only tolerate listening for so long. Other people move on with their lives, but you are left with your grief. So where can you go to keep talking?

THERAPY

Obviously, as a psychotherapist, I have a strong bias in favor of therapy. Therapy gives you a place where, one or more times a week, you can go and talk about your feelings. You can be as depressed, or as angry, or as anxious as you need to be and it will be accepted. In this safe environment you are free to talk about the death, to talk about your loved one, and to talk about your feelings. Healing can occur in therapy because there you can give unlimited expression to your feelings.

While individual therapy can be wonderfully important, group therapy, in the form of a bereavement support group, is absolutely one of the best ways to have your experience validated. You communicate with other people who know what it's like to lose someone. You connect to people in a unique way, on a gut level, and discover that you're not alone in your sorrow. The group provides you with a special place to talk out your grief with people who understand what you are going through because they too are traveling along the same road.

Suse still participates in a "Victims of Pan Am 103" support group, made up of relatives of people who died in that terrible tragedy. Currently approximately three hundred people meet, every other month, and they circulate a newsletter as well. Suse says it was an irony to be "lucky" enough to have a ready-made support group like this. What a terrible price to pay to be so "lucky." But in this group, the members relate in a way that would be impossible with anyone else.

Most people of course don't have such a ready-made support team, but there are other options. You can look for support groups in churches, synagogues, local chapters of national self-help organizations, community centers, mental health clinics, hospitals. Ask the funeral director for a referral. Ask friends. Don't stop until you find one, and if all else fails, start your own group. Candy Lichtner started Mothers Against Drunk Driving (MADD) after her daughter was killed by a drunk driver, and now it has local chapters across the country.

As you begin to heal, a support group is helpful on another level too: it gives you the opportunity to get out of yourself by listening to others' pain and perhaps offering them help. Judith, whose husband died after twenty-five years of marriage, found a support group to be extremely therapeutic in that way. "To me, the important thing about support groups is that it takes the emphasis off of yourself; when you're focusing on other people and listening to their concerns and trying to think of ways to help them, somehow it just is not so heavy for yourself."

The concept of getting out of yourself is an important one.

However, as you will see in chapter 7, it is most powerfully applied in the latter stages of grief. In the beginning of the grieving process, a definite period of self-absorption, of introversion, is necessary. In some ways, you have to be completely, narcissistically involved in order to activate the healing process. You're not really in a position to give to others until you give to yourself first. For example, Eliza, whose eight-month-old baby died in utero, experienced this phenomenon when, just eight weeks after her own loss, she tried to help another woman who had just lost a baby by stillbirth. She told me, "My rabbi asked me if I would visit her. I was looking forward to meeting somebody who I could get out of myself for, to get away from my self-pity and be helpful to her. I would try to tell her it was okay and then I would break down and realize it wasn't okay. We were so caught up in our own grief at first, that we really couldn't help each other."

The point is that in the beginning, in the stage of Disorganization, things are not okay. Life is not fine. You are not doing all right. Someone you loved dearly, someone precious to you, has been wrested from you, and your life is left in shreds. If someone describes a griever to me by saying, "Oh, she's so strong and together; she's handling her grief really well," that's when I worry. I think someone is handling her grief well if I hear that "she's terribly upset, she's crying constantly, she's falling apart." Emotion isn't the problem to be fixed; it's the natural response and the ultimate solution.

EXPRESSION

Not everyone is at ease with being verbal. Men, for example, are often not as free with words as women are. Certain cultures aren't as comfortable with verbal expression as well. Fortunately, other therapeutic ways to express oneself can help.

R. Benyamin Cirlin, a bereavement specialist with the Jacob Perlow Hospice in New York City, says that an important way to cope with grief is "having an outlet, some kind of outlet, be it interpersonal, be it artistic, that will allow the person to not have to contain their grief but will give them an opportunity to express it, to externalize it to some degree."

I think that writing is one of the most immediate and tangible ways to do this. I almost always recommend to my patients that they write if they can. Keep a diary or journal to record your thoughts and feelings and to chart your journey. Write a letter to your deceased loved one about how life is without her, how angry you are that she left, how much you miss her. Write a letter to your grief and tell it how much you hate it, how terrified you are of it, how dreadful it is. Write a letter from your grief to you and see what grief has to tell you. Write down your dreams or a stream of consciousness to release some energy.

You can use writing to your advantage in many ways. One griever I spoke with wrote a play about his brother's murder. He used this as a device to process the magnitude of what had occurred and to establish a sense of control and mastery over a situation that was uncontrollable. Although he's not a professional writer, for him, writing was a way of overcoming the state of helplessness he experienced.

There are many other forms of creative expression besides writing, such as dance, painting, sculpture, singing, playing an instrument, or drawing. Everyone has a unique form that speaks best to him or her. Find some way you're comfortable with to express what you are experiencing. Suse, who is a professional sculptor, naturally looked to this medium to help her cope with her pain after her son died in the Pan Am crash. She found it helpful to literally give shape and form to her feelings. She started out by making sculptures of herself in different feeling states.

Well, right after Alexander died, I felt like I needed to express what was happening inside of me after losing him. I thought what other way but to portray myself, a mother whose child was murdered. So I started by doing what I felt—raging, whimpering, not wanting to know or hear or feel or see—you know, like the monkeys that sit there and cover up everything. So I did a number of mother figures portraying myself.

She told another mother in the group about what she was doing and asked her if she wanted to participate. Soon other women were coming to her asking if they could be a part of the project. So what started as a coping mechanism for Suse quickly became an all-encompassing project. She asked the women to come into her studio and assume the pose they took the moment that they heard that their loved one died. As you can imagine, the women have assumed a variety of positions all expressing different angles of anguish.

Suse has completed twenty-six larger-than-life-sized sculptures so far and plans to complete another one hundred. She considers this her life's work now. The figures compose an exhibit called "Dark Elegy" and are generally displayed in outdoor public spaces. The effect of the piece is staggering. People everywhere are moved to tears as they see the reflections of pain and horror that these people have experienced.

Of course, Suse is a professional sculptor and her work is now viewed by thousands of people. But you do not need that kind of acclaim for your creativity. The quality of the result is irrelevant. No one will be judging you. It's the unique creative expression that is important because it gives voice to feelings that might otherwise be left latent.

RITUALS AND CEREMONIES

Not everyone feels that verbal or creative arts are right for them. I once was lecturing to a group of high school students about bereavement. I was expounding on and on about the virtues of talking and artistic expression, when a young Chinese woman raised her hand and said, "What do you do if you don't like to talk too much and you're not comfortable writing or doing art?" I found myself scrambling to answer her question, because most of the standard techniques in grief work involve these forms of expression. However, other forms of expression can be quite beneficial.

Some cultures and religions have built-in rituals to acknowledge various stages of your loss. However, for many of us, after the funeral, there are none. I recommend creating your own. The best time for a small ritual is any important occasion or anniversary, such as your loved one's birthday or death day. You should set aside time on these special days. Visit the cemetery. Plan a small ceremony that includes some music, a reading, a prayer, sharing a special memory, looking through pictures. The purpose is to set aside special time to remember your loved one and to acknowledge your ongoing loss.

As you work through the grief, you can also devise rituals

to help you release certain emotions. For example, if you find yourself stuck in guilt, you might devise a simple ceremony focusing on forgiveness. You can metaphorically fill a box with your feelings and literally bury it. Or create some personal, meaningful act of atonement. Or you can design a symbolic gesture of new life and love, like planting a tree in your loved one's honor. This kind of ritual is therapeutic and ultimately redemptive. The feelings will not be purged completely but you might feel a perceptible shift in your mourning process.

FOCUS INSIDE

Of course, even as it's important to talk with others, to share, to connect, to do, to be active, to be out there with your grief, it's equally important in working through the stage of Disorganization to be alone, to withdraw, and to focus inside. For now, you need to draw in. Make an appointment with your grief. One suggestion is to set aside a specific time each day for grieving, even if it's just five or ten minutes. You can use that time to sit quietly, review what you're experiencing, let the feelings wash over you, cry. You might be afraid that if you let yourself feel the feelings and cry, you will drown in your own tears and the torrent will never cease. But actually, the feelings, like the tears, will ebb and flow. The waves of emotion may crash over you like a tidal wave, but eventually, the surf recedes.

Let yourself lie fallow for a while. Allow yourself to be lost. Embrace the feelings. Look at them squarely. Allow yourself to indulge in whatever feeling comes up. Let it be. Take it in. Allow the feeling to become part of you. Don't resist it. Surrender to it. Give yourself permission to *feel*. Studies show that people who resist pain are actually in more pain. In other words, your fear of the feeling can be as painful as the actual feeling. Ease into it. Let it become part of you. Laura, whose boyfriend was killed in the automobile accident, said that grief had a life of its own that had to be taken care of; for her, that meant learning to "honor the grief." She tells other grievers to "let however you feel be. Give whatever time and space it needs."

During this quiet time, you might want to read inspirational literature. You might also want to pray or recite positive affirmations. Find what works for you. Meditation is an especially useful tool for helping you get in touch with your feelings. There are many excellent manuals that can teach you how to progressively relax, focus on your breathing, and meditate. Meditation can help you embrace your pain rather than resist it. In fact, studies have shown that meditation aids in combating chronic physical pain by helping people manage and work with the pain rather than fight it. You cannot erase what has happened, but by working with your grief, you can change your relationship to it.

SPIRITUALITY

Spirituality and religion are extremely complicated concepts that we will explore in greater detail later in the book. But for now, in the stage of Disorganization, spirituality can be helpful in several ways. First, if you belong to a church or synagogue, you might find comfort there. Talking to a minister, rabbi, or priest may offer some immediate consolation. Eliza found, after her infant child died, that she was helped by the presence of her rabbi at her side in the hospital. "He was new to the synagogue and I didn't even know him. But he came to the hospital at 11:30 P.M. I was incredibly touched that he came in person to answer our questions. He heard we had a tragedy and he rushed right over to help. It really meant a lot to us."

Some people do not belong to any organized religion but nonetheless may find their faith to be comforting. Andrew said that after John died of AIDS, his faith came through for him. "I needed my faith in God after John died. I needed to rely on it heavily. It was there for me and I was very happy that I had something to believe in, because that's what got me through a lot of it, the initial part of it."

One griever told me that he has "fair-weather spirituality"—whenever things look bleak, he chooses to believe in some guidance, but if things are going fine, he doesn't believe. If your faith or religious connections bring you comfort and strength, then accept it as a blessing. For many people, "fair-weather spirituality" means that when the wind blows trouble, faith is shaken. The spiritual doubts and questions that may arise as a result of the death of your loved one are difficult; we will explore this complex issue more in chapter 10, "Spiritual Doubt and Conflict."

TAKE A BREAK

Yes, often you will need to take a much-needed break. No one can sustain intense feelings twenty-four hours a day. An important survival skill is to give yourself occasional escapes. Go shopping, see a movie, knit, call a friend, take a class on a subject you know nothing about, read a novel, take up a new hobby, cook, flip through a magazine. Do anything that will help you escape the pain for a while.

Lose yourself in exercise: walk, jog, swim, or stretch. Exercise clears the mind and strengthens the body. Even if you do not think of yourself as athletic, just a walk around the block can do wonders. One woman began taking a daily morning walk after her husband of twenty-five years died. She said that doing so made her feel better and it also made her notice nature around her. She watched the trees change from season to season. She found herself able to appreciate something beautiful in the midst of her pain. And certainly, aerobic activity is known to release endorphins, the body's natural painkiller, into your bloodstream so that you just feel better. Furthermore, you'll be healthier as you grieve. As you know by now, grieving takes physical and emotional stamina, and exercise helps you develop both of these. Many of the people I spoke with testified to the healing and calming properties that exercise provided for them.

Use humor for comic relief: watch a funny movie or listen to a comic. Many of the people with whom I spoke commented on the value of humor for easing a wounded heart. In fact, Norman Cousins testifies to the strong tonic of humor in *Anatomy of an Illness*, when he recounts his story of battling a degenerative illness by watching "Candid Camera" reruns and Marx Brothers movies. Jolie, a seventeen-year-old-girl whose father died five years ago, said she sometimes uses humor to lighten a heavy situation. Whenever someone asks her what her father does for a living, she tells them, "He plays the harp with angels outside the pearly gates." And then she laughs. It reminds me of the expression, "Angels can fly because they take themselves lightly."

Just remember, while you definitely need breaks from your grief, your main task in the phase of Disorganization is to acknowledge and express the myriad feelings jumbled within you. Yes, it will be difficult. In fact, it may be one of the greatest challenges you will ever face. It takes a tremendous amount of courage and discipline to actively engage in grief work. Some days you will not have the strength and that's fine too. Take it slowly, take it gently, take it at your own pace. Be patient and kind with yourself. Remember that grief cannot be devoured all at once. It must be digested slowly, in tiny, bite-sized pieces. You have been forced to embark on this journey and there's no turning back.

CHAPTER 3

Rebuilding a Life: Reconstruction

To every thing there is a season,
and a time for every purpose under Heaven:
A time to be born, and a time to die; . . .
A time to break down, and a time to build up;
A time to weep, and a time to laugh;
A time to mourn, and a time to dance . . .
—*ECCLESIASTES 3:1–4*

An old adage holds that grief must be experienced in each of the four seasons before true healing can begin. For many people, the first year of grief is the hardest, as each important holiday, anniversary, and birthday passes without the loved one's presence. The actual date that your loved one died, the death day, becomes charged with significance as well. Confronting the first anniversary of the death day can be a major psychological challenge. In general, the first six to twelve months are recognized as months of "acute" grief, although as we will discuss later, for many people, acute grief takes many years to surface.

But let's assume that you have fully allowed yourself to go through Shock and Disorganization; you have been experiencing the emotions—all of the pain, depression, loneliness, anxiety, anger, guilt. You have turned inward to absorb, process, and face the painful feelings that grief elicits. But what next? You can't remain in the stage of Disorganization indefinitely. You have to begin to function again. As one griever said, "I wanted to go into seclusion like Jackie O. and have everything be better when I came out of seclusion. But it didn't work that way. I still had to go to work, deal with people, be in the real world."

The real world means you have to continue going to work, paying the bills, buying the groceries, raising the children. Life doesn't give you much of a grace period for dealing with acute grief, so the third stage, Reconstruction, actually begins to seep in slowly from the very beginning. You function, you go through the motions of living. At first only tentatively but later with more conviction, you gradually begin to cement together that which has come unglued.

What can you expect in this stage of Reconstruction? Initially, it's just pure distraction from the grimmer moments of Disorganization. You focus, for a moment, on the stack of bills on your desk instead of on your anger. You manage to get to the store for milk and bread. Gradually, Reconstruction stretches to encompass the moments, hours, and, later, days of feeling better. Over time, there are fewer periods of agony and more spaces in your life for pleasure, even happiness. You may think of the deceased person less often, which could make you feel guilty at first. But life begins to resume its pace as you slowly reenter the social and emotional fabric of society. Essentially you rebuild your life from the ground up.

The primary healing goal for this stage is to adjust to a new world, a world without your loved one. This happens on two levels—physical and psychological. On a concrete level it means sifting through his possessions—books, clothing, papers. It means moving his things out so that you have the entire closet for yourself. It means turning her bedroom into a study. And on an emotional/psychological level, it means holding your loved one in your heart but moving on to a new life.

Physical Reconstruction

The physical reconstruction of bereavement occurs slowly. You may focus on minor details of living right away, but it could take awhile before you actually have the energy to face sorting through his things.

I often hear grievers talk about how traumatic it is to face these very physical yet emotionally exhausting tasks. A member of one of my bereavement groups proclaimed one week, "Well, I finally did it; it has taken me eight months, but I cleaned out his side of the closet. I spent the entire weekend sobbing my eyes out. He had saved every card that I ever gave him—that's thirteen years of cards for every occasion. Those, of course, I will save. But I made piles and piles for Goodwill, other piles to put in storage, some stuff to give to friends. I wasn't ready to do this before, but now that I've done it, I feel somehow purged." Bear in mind that it can be a long time before you're ready to face this physical reconstruction, and that you shouldn't force it until you're ready.

I once led a workshop for a group of employees who had lost one of their colleagues, a man who had worked at the company for twenty years. One of the concerns—besides, of course, grieving the loss of their friend and coworker—was the issue of cleaning out his office. This act of physical reconstruction was causing everyone real emotional distress. They couldn't get past the feeling that it was "his" office. The thought of cleaning out the files, "his" stuff, was overwhelming to everyone. And the idea of giving the office to someone else was intolerable.

Part of the goal of the workshop was to normalize their feelings and to give them a chance to process the concerns that many of them had but few of them had shared. They took their time, respecting the need to honor the process. Several months later, I heard that they had finally cleaned out his office and had scheduled a new employee to move into it. The feeling afterward was one of relief and closure.

Often people exclaim that, although the process of physical reconstruction can be bittersweet, once it is completed a sense of calm and peace often settles in. In a sense, these physical reconstructions are like rituals that close certain chapters in our lives. They are symbolic of the need to move on.

One woman I worked with lost her best friend, her soul mate. Although she didn't live with him, she had always had an intense, emotionally close relationship with him. In his will, he entrusted to her the task of distributing his ashes to four selected special friends. He had left her with detailed instructions about how to execute the distribution.

It was months before she could even contemplate carrying out this directive. She said that she couldn't bring herself to do it because she was afraid it would be like losing him again.

She didn't want to let go. Yet during the course of our eight-week support group, she began to feel the strength she needed to face the task and to let go. The other group members encouraged her desire to complete the task.

One week she came in and told us, "I have something important to share with the group. I finally distributed his ashes." Everyone murmured their support. She went on to say that the weekend was emotional and many tears were shed, but that she knew she was doing what her friend wanted her to do. And furthermore, she now had a sense of almost relief. She said, "I know it seems funny, but I actually feel lighter, somehow. I didn't expect it, but I really feel lighter, like it's easier to walk and easier to breathe."

Holding on expends a great deal of emotional energy. The stages of letting go and moving on cause an actual emotional lightening as energy is redirected back to life.

Rebuilding physically also means addressing the secondary losses that you have experienced. In other words, you didn't just lose your wife, you lost your bookkeeper, chef, and social organizer. So you learn new roles or activities that you might not have been responsible for before. For example, your wife used to pay all the bills and now you must learn to do this. Or your husband did all the grocery shopping and cooking and now you will have to take over these responsibilities.

A common time for discovering secondary losses is around the holidays. Perhaps you always used to visit your daughter at Christmas and now must make other arrangements. Or you suddenly realize that it was your father who always bought presents for your aunt, now you'd better. You'll be discovering new secondary losses for quite some time. And each time you discover one, it will hit you all over again, freshly, painfully, that your loved one is truly gone.

Psychological Reconstruction

Knowing that special people are gone means you must rebuild your life on a psychological level. You learn that you cannot go to your loved ones for advice anymore. They're no longer available for phone calls, moral support, a cup of coffee. You reconstruct a life with their memory, but without their presence. You experience more of an internalized understanding that your loved one is gone and is not coming back. Essentially, you accept the fact that your loved one has died, and you decide to move on.

Sally is a widow in her early sixties. She was married to Dan for thirty-one years. They had a lovely life together, along with their two grown children. Dan died suddenly, completely unexpectedly, just two days before they were to leave on an extended summer vacation to Italy.

Sally was in shock for several months. But when Disorganization finally hit, it hit forcefully. She retreated. She stayed in bed for days. She cried for months on end. She joined a widows' group and immersed herself in the feelings of Disorganization. She forced herself to visit all the places that she and Dan had ever gone. And her tears continued.

Sally might have easily gotten stuck in Disorganization, she might have easily gotten blocked by the pain. After all, for thirty-one years Dan had been her "right arm." They had an entire past behind them as well as an entire future laid out before them. She avoided getting stuck, however; she managed to stay with her feelings, she allowed her grief to run its course (the timing of which is different for everybody), and then she started becoming aware of the need to consciously move "beyond bereavement."

After Dan died, after I grieved, I focused on a large white sheet of paper, and it was entitled, "What am I going to do for the rest of my life?" and it was blank. I didn't know how to write one sentence on that big white sheet. I had had the whole rest of my life planned with Dan. I had had a blueprint for the rest of my life—living in Florida, vacations, details. I couldn't write the first sentence for over a year. I kept saying, "What am I going to do with my life?" No one could tell me that. No book, no widows' group, nobody could say.

I guess I finally came up with the concept that I don't really have the rest of my life. I just dropped it and focused on the value of small goals. I trained myself to focus on one season at a time. I know I've got plans for the spring, then the summer. But I don't know what my fall is yet. In June, I will think about my fall.

Dan is still a part of her life, but Sally has moved past her grief; she moved through Disorganization to the other side of pain.

The tears have changed in their complexion, it's a softer, warmer tear. At times I still feel sad, and I'll go to the cemetery to talk to Dan. I tease him and chat with him. [But now] I bring an air of lightness or humor to life and I ease into even bad situations, which

I didn't used to do. I used to be very serious, "we've got to solve this, this matters," but that's all gone.

The actual grieving comes to an end almost imperceptibly. The best way to shake something is to stay with it. If you accept it, you will diffuse it. If you try to push it away, it gains power. Once I got better, I initially felt guilty. I thought, "I can't be better." I still missed him but in a different way, a healthy way. I was able to miss him in a way that didn't tear me apart.

Incidentally, when last I heard from Sally, she was spending several months of the year living in a beach house. She was leading "Beyond Bereavement" workshops for widows at a local community center. And she was seriously dating another man. Sally accepted the need to move on and subsequently made a new blueprint for her life.

Acceptance

Many people are familiar with Elisabeth Kübler-Ross's book *On Death and Dying*. Published in 1969, it is still considered a seminal book in the field of thanatology, the study of death-related subjects. She was one of the first people to openly discuss a very taboo subject—death. She worked with dying patients and identified a five-stage process that dying patients experience: denial, anger, bargaining, depression, and acceptance. The idea behind these stages developed in her work with *dying* patients, not grievers.

The process for a dying person differs from that of a grieving person. It makes sense that a dying patient will first deny his diagnosis, then be angry about it, then bargain for his life, then realize that he must die anyway and thus feel depressed, and ultimately come to accept that he will die. There is a finality to this process since he does, in fact, eventually die. For the person left in death's wake, for the griever, this process is not exactly accurate; it doesn't wholly match the experience. Yes, there may be denial at first, and certainly lots of anger and depression, but it does not *end* with acceptance. The grieving process does not have a final event built into it.

In bereavement, people experience different levels of acceptance at different points in the process. First is the acceptance necessary as the healing goal of the Shock stage, that is, breaking through the denial of the death and accepting the reality that your loved one did in fact die. This must be followed by the task, in Disorganization, of accepting the feelings. In Reconstruction, the task of acceptance requires coming to terms physically and psychologically with the reality that your loved one has died, in an acknowledgment of both the death and the need to move on.

Acceptance does not mean that you *like* what happened, nor does it mean that you forget your loved one. It means that you understand the magnitude of what has happened, knowing that your life will never be the same, knowing that you must learn to live with the loss.

Another key element of acceptance is coming to grips with all that your loved one was, the good and the not-so-good parts, the happy memories and the sad memories—accepting, in other words, the reality of the person you lost.

Idealization

It is not uncommon, in the midst of memorializing the deceased, to actually idealize this beloved person. We have a saying that we shouldn't speak ill of the dead . . . nor think ill, nor remember ill things. If you remember negative things about this person, you feel guilty, even foolish. So suddenly all the normal personality flaws that were very evident in life get airbrushed by death.

But let's face it, nobody's perfect. Dysfunctional relationships with your parents, the seeds of which were sown in childhood, may account for many of your current relationship problems. And consider that the divorce rate is still 50 percent. Consider also the strains of sibling rivalry that grow and flourish over a lifetime. Every relationship has some conflict—after all, we're not living in a Frank Capra movie.

A big part of psychological reconstruction is letting go of any idealized vision of your loved one and allowing yourself to remember more of the real human being who lived, complete with imperfections. Whereas in the stage of Disorganization it was normal to idealize your beloved since that brought you comfort, in this stage you allow for the fact that your loved one wasn't perfect. You accept all of the many facets of who he was. You embrace the reality of who he was in life, and you accept the reality of who he is now in death.

I once led a workshop for a group of women who had lost their mothers. As I was describing the need to release idealization, one woman tentatively raised her hand. When I called on her, she quietly said, "But my mother *was* perfect."

A few women in the audience smiled. I simply asked, "How old were you when your mother died?" She answered, "I was eight." I replied, "That explains it. To an eight-year-old, your mother *was* perfect. If your mother had lived until you were fifteen, I bet you wouldn't remember her as being so perfect." She laughed and nodded her head in agreement.

That's not to say that people aren't wonderful, because they are. And your beloved certainly could have been generous, loving, funny, giving, honest, and so on. Certainly he had more fabulous traits than difficult ones, which is why you loved him in the first place. But still, he wasn't *perfect*. No one is. Coming to accept the full spectrum of who your dear one was, coming to embrace the totality—the entire package deal—is the hallmark of healthy grieving.

The danger of clinging to an idealized image is that it most likely masks a deeper conflict blocked by pain and ambivalence. And whenever unconscious blocks of this nature occur, they prevent emotional growth and development. In other words, holding onto an idealized, and therefore unrealistic, view covers over a deeper unconscious conflict and thus prevents you from moving forward. Chapter 11, "Complicated Grief," looks at this type of problem in more depth. The point to remember now is to allow the process of Reconstruction into your life, and that includes reconstructing a realistic memory of your loved one. The process occurs gradually, imperceptibly.

The Balance

The boundary between Disorganization and Reconstruction is not distinct. A person commonly experiences both stages simultaneously, although in different measure. It's the ratio between them that is the critical element. For example, in the first several months, you might experience mostly Disorganization but some Reconstruction in your life. That's normal and necessary. Over time, you reach more Reconstruction and less Disorganization. Occasionally you might "relapse" for a while, but in time, without having witnessed the slow change, you will wake up and realize that the ratio has again moved closer to mostly Reconstruction with a little less Disorganization. Once again: it's a process.

Think of it like a balance scale. In the beginning, the Disorganization side has most, but not all of the weight. Over time the scale is tipped so that the Reconstruction side has most, but not all of the weight. It may waver back and forth, in a seesaw motion, for some time. This is normal, but eventually Reconstruction will outweigh Disorganization.

Unfortunately there is no formula for predicting when the scale will begin to tilt to the side of mostly Reconstruction. For each person, the balancing act differs. You cannot have one intense moment, an epiphany, and then be done with Disorganization forever. On average, it takes one to three years to work through the Disorganization phase after a major loss. That's because you need to process your grief repeatedly so that it can sink in, settling on deeper levels of consciousness over time. Depending on many circumstances, it could take less time, or much more.

Nonetheless, after you've reconstructed, after you've moved on, after you've accepted, you're not just done with your grief. On a very important level, your grief work will never be "finished," because your loss will always be a part of you. That is why in the model that I work with, after Shock, Disorganization, and Reconstruction, I include two more stages—Synthesis and Transcendence—and each of these stages deals specifically with grief's ongoing impact in your life. These stages, described in part 2, are dynamic, fluid, continuous life stages that you will now be grappling with on an ongoing basis.

PART II

The Lifelong Impact of Grief

CHAPTER 4

Integrating Life with Loss: Synthesis

Your joy is your sorrow unmasked.
And the selfsame well from which your
laughter rises was oftentimes filled with your tears.
And how else can it be?
The deeper that sorrow carves into your
being, the more joy you can contain.
—KAHLIL GIBRAN

One fifty-eight-year-old widow told me that after her husband died, she was searching for answers and was hungry for information. She read every grief book she could get her hands on and attended lectures on bereavement. One speaker, she said, told a room full of widows that, "Your husband now is nothing more than mementos in a scrapbook. You must accept this fact and move on with your life." This widow said, "I was so outraged that he had the nerve to say such a thing. I mean how incredibly harsh to say that to a room full of widows. My husband is just part of a scrapbook, and that's it? I have to accept that and be done with it?"

A popular belief holds that after a major loss, you can grieve it, accept it, and be done with it. Sigmund Freud promoted this idea in his influential paper "Mourning and Melancholia," explaining that for grief to be resolved, emotional energy must be withdrawn from the deceased and reinvested in something new. This is true *to a certain extent*. Freud, however, went further and postulated that one must "decathect" energy, that is, one must sever the tie, end the relationship. In other words, as the speaker told the widows, your beloved must become nothing more than scraps in a scrapbook.

My position is that you cannot and should not sever the ties. Your loved one is in your heart, in your soul, and wrapped intrinsically into who and what you are. You will spend the rest of your life remembering, internalizing, and renegotiating all that this loss means to you in this lifetime. Just because the person is dead, it doesn't mean that your feelings or the relationship dies. This lifelong stage of integration and reworking, which I call Synthesis, accounts for the fact that even after dozens of years have passed, grievers are still affected by their loss. Synthesis accounts for the fact that you will always and forever have a relationship to your deceased loved one. Synthesis accounts for the fact that you will never be quite the same person as you were before, for better or for worse. Society's common misconception is that grieving can be completed within a few months if not weeks, and that then life resumes. But grief's reality is that life is forever changed, you are forever changed, and you will continue to reprocess your grief throughout the years.

Perhaps this is not something you want to hear. Perhaps

you would prefer that I offer you a ten-session course in recovery guaranteed to complete your grieving process so that you can return to the way things were. Perhaps you, like everyone else you talk to, want to find a quick fix, take a pill, and be done with this. But I can't offer you that. If you sit quietly and listen to your inner voice, if you allow yourself to hear its truth, you will know that this is forever.

I'm not saying that the searing pain is forever—because, believe it or not, that will heal. The agony of acute feelings will fade. And I'm not saying that you cannot or should not move on, for you do eventually have to withdraw energy from the deceased and channel it back into something meaningful. Indeed, the final stage of grief work, Transcendence, is one of growth. It is all about finding ways to move on creatively and to make meaning out of loss. What I am saying, however, is that the impact, the impression, the imprint of grief has and will continue to change your life. The healing goal in the stage of Synthesis is to recognize that you will always be influenced by this loss—just as you will always be influenced by the love you shared—and thus you need to establish an ongoing relationship with your grief and with your beloved.

You may be asking, then, "What precisely does it mean? If I proceed through Shock and Disorganization, and I tackle the tasks of Reconstruction in my life, then what exactly can I expect in this ongoing, lifelong process of Synthesis?"

Synthesis comprises four important concepts: *retriggering*, *connection*, *memory*, and *dialogue*. The first two of these components of Synthesis deal with your ongoing relationship with your loss, and the second two components deal with your ongoing relationship with your loved one.

Retriggering

Life will continue to go on and at times you will think you are "finished" with your grief; "Oh, I'm over this now," you may say to yourself. But life has ways of bringing the loss back to you, it reminds you at certain checkpoints, and you may be astonished that the pain and other feelings can flood back to you so quickly, as if it all happened yesterday. Certain days, certain life transitions, certain sensory impressions all have the ability to bring the loss back to you.

Holidays, birthdays, death days, anniversaries, and life ceremonies can and do reopen the wound and remind the griever of her loss. For example, Judy's father died when she was eighteen. Now thirty-one, she told me she felt that she had grieved adequately and had spent many years processing the grief. She had successfully moved on with her life. But as she was planning her wedding with her fiancé, thirteen years after her father's death, she was surprised and over-whelmed to realize that her father's death felt so close. "I keep coming back to the fact that he won't be there to walk me down the aisle or dance at my wedding. I thought I was prepared for this, I really did. But he's not going to be there for this, and it just hurts so much. I'm amazed at how fresh the pain feels and how the loss can still affect me this deeply after all these years."

Hope Edelman, author of the hugely successful *Motherless Daughters*, and a motherless daughter herself, talks about how for a woman who loses her mother, certain developmental life points may retrigger feelings of grief. For example, if a young woman loses her mother when she is fourteen, say, and her mother forty-four, this young woman may find that grief is retriggered during developmental stages and life transitions: when she graduates from high school and college, when she gets married, when she becomes a mother, when she turns forty-four herself—Hope Edelman calls this the neon number—the exact age her own mother was when she died. This woman may also have a retriggering when her own daughter reaches fourteen years—the age she herself was when her mother died. In this instance, the adult daughter identifies simultaneously with the daughter who loses the mother as well as with the mother who would have left a fourteen-year-old daughter.

Hope, who lost her mother when she was seventeen, told me, "As I was doing the interviews [for the book], I had the same themes coming up over and over again—fear of getting the mother's illness, fear of dying at the same age that she did, a longing for her at the transitional times in a woman's life, but most importantly the sense that nobody got over the loss of a mother in six months, or a year, or even five years . . . that these were women who still clearly were mourning the loss of their mothers even though they had gone on in every other respect to have very happy and productive and fulfilling lives. That was a source of great encouragement to me. I started to get a sense that what I was feeling could be characterized as 'normal' long-term grief."

Sometimes sounds, or smells, or even places will remind you of the loss. One griever commented that when his son died, there were helicopters in the air for some unrelated reason. He said that now, wherever he is and whatever he's doing, if he hears a helicopter, it brings it all back—all the feelings and emotions—as if it were yesterday. That yesterday was twenty-two years ago. Another griever lost her brother while she and her family were living temporarily in

Italy. This griever said that not only is it difficult and emotional to ever visit Italy again, she even feels pangs of grief when she eats Italian food. "It's amazing that after so many years, just the smell of lasagna throws me back to that time and place and remembering how unbearable it was to lose Thomas."

It is normal to experience these retriggerings, these reverberations, for the rest of your life. Some of them you can plan for, like holidays or birthdays. Some you will develop rituals for, such as visiting the grave site every year on the death day, or lighting a candle every year on the deceased's birthday. Others will catch you unaware and leave you feeling bewildered and slightly confused.

For example, you may find yourself inexplicably depressed, feeling lethargic, having trouble sleeping, not knowing why. After some reflection, some talking, perhaps even some therapy, you discover that there is some connection with the death. One father I spoke with lost his eight-year-old son Jeremy in a bizarre accident just over thirteen years ago. This past spring, the father was experiencing nightmares and a depression when he realized that his son would have been graduating from college just now. He couldn't help but reexperience the loss anew, wondering what it would have been like, what his son would be doing, what he would have studied and what career he would be pursuing. The reverberations rebound and echo throughout a lifetime.

The Dougy Center in Portland, Oregon has a unique way of helping people recognize this fact. Through the supportive/therapeutic weeks and weekends it offers, in a camplike setting, the center helps bereaved children and parents cope with their losses. Staff members understand the essence of retriggering, that while you will move on and grow and heal, there will always be days that are tinged with pain and bring back the loss anew. Thus, upon "graduation," they present each client with a bag of beautifully polished stones. But one of the stones in the bag is purposely left rough and jagged to remind the griever that while many days ahead will be beautiful and polished, there will still be some rough days as well. That is part of the normal grieving process.

Connection

It is a well-established and well-known phenomenon in bereavement theory that every death stirs up previous losses, especially unresolved losses. All losses are connected. I imagine them like beads strung on a string, and as a new loss is added, it slides along the strand, bumping the most recent bead and sending ripples throughout the whole line. So from this day forward, every future loss you experience will subtly resurrect this loss—just as this loss has subtly (or sometimes not so subtly) resurrected previous losses.

That's why, if you don't do the grief work now, there will be ample opportunity to do so later, because this grief work will be coming around again and again and again.

Vicky is a forty-four-year-old woman whose boyfriend of fourteen years was brutally murdered in his own apartment in 1986. Her boyfriend, Alan, was a drug user and Vicky believes that one of Alan's "friends" murdered him in a drug-related argument. You can imagine how difficult it has been for Vicky to process her anger, the horror of the violence, the complications inherent in a murder case.

But Vicky discovered that not only was she responding to

the very real, painful, overwhelming, violent loss of her lover, but that she also was responding to the distant, buried, unresolved loss of her father, who died when Vicky was twelve years old. When she was a child, her family didn't encourage her to grieve her father's death. This is not uncommon because adults mistakenly think that if they shield their children from grief, they are somehow protecting them from pain.

I never mourned when my father died. My family told me, "You're not supposed to cry; you're supposed to be strong." I remember telling my mother that I wanted to see a therapist but she said, "We don't do that in our family." The message was you're supposed to bear your grief and get on with it. I don't remember interacting with my mom at all. She would come home from work and hide in her bed. One week after my dad died, I was sent away to be with relatives at the New Jersey shore for the summer. I didn't know how to react. I was supposed to be having a good time on the beach, but my father had just died. Nobody talked about it. They thought it would be good for me to get away from the mourning. I cried myself to sleep every night. But I was never allowed to grieve openly.

Vicky said that her suppressed mourning probably contributed to the fact that she later had problems with men, afraid that they were all going to abandon her. She became cynical about life. She said, "Your parents are supposed to be around forever, especially to a twelve-year-old girl." Her denied grief may have even unconsciously contributed to her becoming involved with Alan, a man twenty-two years her senior, a man old enough to be her father.

In Synthesis, Vicky discovered that not only did she have to integrate her boyfriend's death into her life, but also her father's death.

> Between my father and Alan, there was a lot to deal with. I suddenly had to deal with all that stuff I never confronted when I was twelve years old. [Alan's death] brought up all of that. I had never mourned my father the first time. I finally learned that it was okay to have feelings and emotions. I got into therapy and gave myself permission to actually *feel*. It seemed self-indulgent at first but I realized I didn't need to be one hundred percent okay. I was shocked at the depth and intensity of my feelings, but you see, I was really grieving two deaths. An astrologer told me that I didn't deal with grief the first time and now I have another chance. There are no shortcuts.

It took Vicky many years to work through her feelings around both of these major losses. She found that she was full of anger and hostility—toward the assailant, toward her boyfriend, toward the criminal justice system, toward the police, toward her father, toward her mother. In fact, after a meditational retreat she attended five years after Alan's death, only then did she begin to let go of the anger. "I finally began to come to terms with the hostility. Holding onto it was destroying me. The anger was so formidable but I just had to release it." She acknowledges that she still has to cope, at times, with the anger. Seven years after the death of her boyfriend and almost thirty years after the death of her father she says she feels she has completed most of her grief work, but "it's always there on some level. Those losses have become integrated into my being and who I am."

The loss you are grieving now is connected to all of your past losses, just as all future losses will be connected to this one. The way in which you grieve for one loss will, in turn, affect how you will grieve for the next. No single loss is experienced in a vacuum. Each will be experienced within the total context of the other losses of your life.

Memory

In Josephine Hart's novel *Oblivion*, the young male protagonist is coping with the loss of his young wife, and the peculiar dilemma of trying to start a new relationship with a new woman. Even as he dates this new woman, he is constantly thinking of his deceased wife. In the novel, the deceased wife is a ghostly character who appears to her mother and talks about fearing a second death, that of sinking into oblivion. She fears that her surviving loved ones—specifically her husband—will forget her.

The deceased wife need not fear being forgotten. Even as the husband goes on to remarry and to have a child, he is constantly thinking of his deceased wife, carrying her presence with him, remembering her. He says, "That's what death does to life, it burns a new pattern on the body, a tattoo of loss. Internal and external loss, etched in acid on your soul, on mind, on memory, . . ."

Perhaps you fear that your beloved will sink into oblivion and that your own memory will fail you. Perhaps you're already discovering that you can't exactly remember how his

voice sounded. Perhaps it's troubling you that you can't recall exactly how she laughed. A griever in my bereavement
group commented, "I still have his voice on our answering
machine even one year later because I can't bear to erase it.
It's the only thing I have with his voice on it. If I lose this,
I'll lose a vital connection with him."

It's true that the memories become dimmer. But it's also
true that the memories persist. Your memories become like
valued archives in your mind. Your loved one's life cannot
be erased, because it lives in the past, it lives in your heart.
Victor Frankl, a psychiatrist who survived the Nazi concentration camps, has written several excellent books on his experiences and his subsequent ideas about human nature. In
Man's Search for Meaning he talks about how the past is a
treasure trove.

> I never tire of saying that the only really transitory
> aspects of life are the potentialities; but as soon as they
> are actualized, they are rendered realities at that mo-
> ment; they are saved and delivered into the past,
> wherein they are rescued and preserved from transito-
> riness. For, in the past, nothing is irretrievably lost but
> everything irrevocably stored. Thus, the transitoriness
> of our existence in no way makes it meaningless. . . .
> Nothing can be undone, and nothing can be done away
> with. I should say *having been* is the surest kind of be-
> ing.

Frankl points out that a life lived becomes poignantly pre-
served for all eternity. An important aspect of Synthesis is
that no one can ever take away your memories. No one can
remove the precious times that you had with your loved one.

These memories are for you to keep, to treasure, to store in the recesses of your mind and heart. The memories will come at expected moments and unexpected ones. Some will bring you sorrow and some will bring you joy and happiness. The memories fuse and synthesize into the you that you are becoming.

Dialogue

The point is becoming clear, I suspect, that your relationship with your loved one is ongoing. Just because your beloved has died, it doesn't mean that your relationship has died too. When a star dies in the universe, its light continues to penetrate the darkness for many millions of years. Our loved ones are like stars in the heavens now, and although their lives have ended on this earth, their lights continue to shine. Their influence endures.

Dialogue is about the ongoing exchanges that you have with the deceased. These happen both on an internal level as well as an external level. One aspect of internal dialogue is taking part of that person into yourself—telling jokes that he used to tell, sharing meaningful stories that he used to recite. You may take on some of his interests or take over roles that he assumed. For example, your dad always used to roast the turkey at Thanksgiving, and now that is your job. You may start hobbies that reflect interests your loved one had. This sort of internal dialogue is a type of identification.

Or you might take on characteristics of your loved one or imagine how he would have felt about or handled a situation. Jamie, whose father died when she was in college, says that one thing that helped her get through her grief was remembering her father and his personality. "I've always tried to keep in mind what he was like, how he enjoyed life. That gives me coping power; it makes me realize that this man loved life to the fullest. He didn't feel sorry for himself; he made the most of what he had and that in a way, gives me strength." Jamie is inspired by her father and absorbs part of his personality into her own. By incorporating the best parts of him, she renews her relationship to him.

Forging this new affiliation is an important task in the Synthesis stage because it allows your loved one to live eternally in your heart. Many people tell me that they converse or talk with their loved one on a regular basis. One woman who lost her father when she was sixteen, almost twenty years ago, told me, "I kind of talk to him the way I might pray to God. I just talk to him, as if he's looking down on me. I once heard an interview with Julia Roberts, who lost her father when she was seven, and she said that in some ways she has an advantage because now he's always there with her. She always has him. That's kind of true for me too. He's with me all the time."

Another aspect of internal dialogue is that you have a chance to renegotiate your relationship with your loved one. That means that you face the unresolved conflicts, arguments, issues that never were sorted out between you. You work on forgiveness, letting go of past hurts. Part of dialogue is making peace with the loose ends, finding spaces for forgiveness in your heart, reviewing what this person was to you and where he fits into your life. This is a process not accomplished quickly or easily, but it is possible to do. In Chapter 11, we will look at specific ways to work through conflicts and complications.

Dialogue that takes external forms is also very helpful to the process of Synthesis. An example of this is keeping up pictures of the departed loved one. Another example is allowing your thoughts of that person to enter your conversations with friends, saying, "Oh, Harold would have loved this restaurant," or "When Sara and I were in Greece together for our fifth wedding anniversary . . ." In other words, you don't pretend that this person never existed. You don't wipe out all the evidence of his or her life. You continue an external dialogue.

One griever told me that for at least a year after his lover's death, when he came home from work and opened the door to his apartment, he called out, "Hi honey, I'm home." On one level he was saying "hello" to the box of ashes on the fireplace mantel. But on another level, he was developing his external dialogue with the presence of his beloved.

Unfortunately our culture doesn't exactly encourage internal or external dialogues. One widow told me that when she went to a dinner party and mentioned her dead husband, she stopped the conversation cold. She said, "People were visibly uncomfortable, as if I had just uttered a string of curses. They cleared their throats, avoided my eyes, and quickly changed the subject." Generally, Western society refrains from ongoing dialogues with the deceased, although certainly progress is being made. That's why things like the Vietnam War memorial and the AIDS quilt are so comforting and important. They recognize the need for memorialization and ongoing dialogue. Consider the gifts and letters that people bring to the memorial and to the grave sites. People are hungry to remember and to dialogue and our country needs to offer outlets for this communication.

*   *   *

Another specific type of external dialogue is quite common yet rarely discussed: literal communication with the ghosts, presences, or spirits of the deceased. Many of the grievers I counsel have these mystical types of experiences. Almost all mention it with a whisper, afraid that they will be perceived as crazy. The types of contacts range from objects that move by themselves, lights turning on and off, visions, messages, or thought communications. It may seem the stuff of a suspense novel, but the stories are so consistent and so typical that they cannot be easily dismissed. As one griever told me, "My brother's death made me realize that the veil that separates us from the dead is so incredibly thin, and every once in a while, there's a tear."

Christina is a sixty-three-year-old woman whose son died unexpectedly from an undiagnosed heart condition. Christina is a deeply religious woman who follows a self-study religious movement called "A Course in Miracles." Christina was shattered after she learned that Robby had died. She said that for five days after his death she walked around her apartment saying, "Where are you, Robby?"

All of a sudden, I got an answer. He said, "Mom, I'm just as shocked and surprised as you are. I had no idea consciously that this would happen." He was like an auditory presence—I didn't see him, but I felt him and I heard him. It was like the dialogue was taking place inside my head. He also said, "I know it seems terrible and seems awful, but everything's in order according to God's plan. It's not really terrible. In fact, Mom, we're closer now than we were before."

He also told me that he was greeted by Jesus who

said to Robby, "You're a beloved child of God, welcome home. I'm proud of you and happy you're here." Robby said he melded into the love and the peace of Jesus. I suppose you could say it's just hallucinations, imagination, or psychosis. I suppose it's possible. But I believe. When I'm available and not distracted, he comes to me. It's so comforting.

Others say that they feel the presence of their loved one working in their lives, that they know he or she is there watching over them. Several people commented on the fact that for a short period after the death, they sensed their loved ones hanging around for a while to be with them, making sure they were okay, guiding them. But they also sensed when their loved ones moved on.

One country that is more accepting of paranormal experiences, a culture definitely not uncomfortable with Dialogue, is Mexico. They have an annual celebration in October, leading up to November 2, "El Día de los Muertos" (the Day of the Dead, which roughly corresponds to our Halloween). This is a festive holiday with age-old traditions that link the living and the dead. It is believed that the spirits of the dead return to earth during this festival to renew bonds of kinship and love. It is a time of celebration and joy, a time of family reunion—both for the living and for the dead.

A major tradition of this holiday is to make an *ofrenda*, or altar, in the home. A table, usually covered with white or embroidered cloth, is laden with special flowers, fruits, foods, and gifts for the dead. The altars are often decorated with special paper decorations, photographs, candles, and other trinkets. Bakeries throughout the country sell special breads

baked in the shapes of skulls and crossbones. Various art-
works, such as pottery, skull figurines, and ornaments also
appear widely at this time.

This holiday is one of happiness and celebration. It is a
time to honor the dead, to dialogue with them, to reminisce
about them with friends and family. Children grow up in
this culture learning that death is a natural part of life and
that ongoing relationships with the dead are expected.

The Japanese also incorporate ongoing dialogue into their
culture. Most every home has an altar or shelf set aside with
stone tablets as a tribute to those in the family who have
died. These are the *ancestors*, and the living must perform
many series of rituals out of respect to the ancestors. The
Japanese also traditionally celebrate the *bon* festival in late
summer when, for three days, the dead return to earth to
visit the living. Many rituals are devised for this time to
welcome the dead back and to facilitate communications
with them.

A Love That Lasts Forever

The reason it's inevitable that you remember and you
continue to dialogue is that you still love this person! Love
is a gift, a gift that you received, and one that you had the
courage to accept. You had the courage to give your heart
away knowing that it might get broken. But the good news
is that love is eternal; it transcends even death. Although the
person died, the love didn't. Nothing can take away the love
that you shared, ever. And nothing can take away the love
that you continue to feel. Ralph Waldo Emerson said it quite
beautifully:

In this universe
   nothing is ever wholly lost.
That which is excellent
   remains forever a part of this universe.
Human hearts are dust,
   but the love which moves the human heart
   abides to bless
   the last generation.

Everything you are today was molded and influenced by the fact that you loved and were loved in return. That love and that influence will forever be a part of who you are. But just as you are a different person today for having loved, you are also a different person now for having lost.

A Loss That Lasts Forever

According to the Alcoholics Anonymous model for alcoholism, an alcoholic can never fully recover from his disease. He can be sober for five, ten, twenty years, but he is still an alcoholic. Why? Because he is still affected by his disease and could easily become a drunk again. Therefore, in AA they say that an alcoholic is recovering but never recovered. Even if the alcoholic never picks up another drink in his life, he is still conscious of the fact that he is an alcoholic.

In much the same way, a griever is recovering and healing, but is never fully recovered. That doesn't mean that you can't heal or move on, just as the alcoholic can in fact be sober for the rest of his life. But the grieving process is lifelong in that the griever will be forever touched and affected by his loss. Florence, whose twenty-two-year-old son died fifteen years ago said, "I have accepted that he's dead, but I still grieve. This grief that goes on is a grief that can continue to be healthy. I cannot deny that I miss him, and I don't want to not miss him. How could I forget him? He was my son. I will always feel sad that he had to die in the prime of his life. The hard part of it will never go away, but neither will the wonderful part of his life and who he was. That's what I hold onto."

In summary, Synthesis reflects that loss is like a deep wound. It heals over time, but it leaves a lasting scar that will, at times, feel sore. With *retriggering*, you will feel pangs for the rest of your life—on anniversaries, holidays, birthdays, death days—all of these will remind you of your loss. It's important to develop rituals to commemorate these days, like visiting the cemetery or saying a special prayer. Certain places, sounds, and smells will also stimulate feelings.

With *connection*, future losses will stimulate this loss, just as this loss stimulated previous losses. Any unresolved issues will be resurrected. Once again, it's never too late to do the grief work, since sweeping it under the rug merely results in a buildup that eventually overflows. Grief continually demands that you engage in a relationship with it. And with *memory* and *dialogue*, your relationship with your loved one will continue to be reworked, revived, and renegotiated. The reality of Synthesis means both bittersweet sorrow, happy memories, and forever being affected by your loss. It means learning to live with the loss for the rest of your life. It means adapting to life with this new circumstance.

But being forever changed isn't all negative. Remember the Chinese symbol for crisis that means both danger and opportunity. Grief can mean new paths of growth, new fuel for living. And that's what finally leads us toward Transcendence.

CHAPTER 5

Making Meaning out of Loss over Time: Transcendence

---

*To the inhabitant of New York, Paris or London,
death is a word that is never uttered because it
burns the lips. The Mexican, on the other hand,
frequents it, mocks it, caresses it, sleeps with it,
entertains it; it is one of his favorite playthings and
his most enduring love.*
—OCTAVIO PAZ

It may at first seem that because Synthesis is a lifelong stage, you will forever be going around in circles, doomed to a dizzying merry-go-round of grief. The first anniversary comes and goes and you are upset; the fifth anniversary comes, your grief is retriggered and you are upset; the twentieth anniversary comes, and yes, you find yourself upset. You may think to yourself, "Haven't I been here before?"

Actually grief does go around in circles, but the circles do not exist on the same plane. Think of grief like a spiral, a coil moving in a vertical direction. The reality is that each revisiting of a feeling or a sensation is on a different level. Processing the grief is about moving up the spiral in a dynamic upward motion, constantly reencountering old material, but never at exactly the same place. The experience of grief is fluid, not static, so reencountering aspects of it will be different, depending on how you are changing and growing. Every time you allow yourself to experience a feeling, the reality of the loss sinks in more deeply, permeating itself into your life on all levels. The repetition is actually generating growth as the movement goes up the spiral because the more the grief is absorbed into your life, the easier it will ultimately be to move on.

Grief is not a mountain that you climb, go over the top, and then climb back down the other side so that you're at the same ground level as when you started. The spiral nature of grief is more like a journey in which you scale the mountain by going around and around the mountain, gradually moving your way up to new heights, but once you finally make it to the top, you're not going back down. You can never go back down.

This journey brings you to a new place, a different place from where you started, for at the top of the spiral, at the peak of the mountain, is a state that I call Transcendence. If autumn, with its fiery, glowing goodbye and blazing breathlessness, represents death and Shock; and winter, with its frigid, barren landscape, represents Disorganization; and spring, with buds blooming and life recycling, represents Reconstruction and Synthesis; then summer is Transcendence—with full blossoms, heady fragrances, and ripe fruit.

Defining Transcendence

"Sounds good, but what actually *is* transcendence?" you ask. Transcendence literally means "to rise above," to be metaphorically lifted up, to have an aerial view and thereby gain a new perspective. For example, if you've ever been to New York City, you'll know that it is a wonderfully crazy, crowded, energetic, and frenetic place. But if you've ever visited the Empire State Building, you get a totally different perspective on the city. As you are physically lifted above it, you see things in a new light; you get a sense of breadth, scope, beauty in the vastness. You're exposed to a broader horizon, and you might never think of the city again in the same way. Having transcended the city, you've reached a different level of experiencing it.

In Transcendence as a stage of advanced healing, perspective is key. Think about how vital a role perspective plays when you view an Impressionist painting. If you stand up close, all you will notice are abstract dashes and daubs of paint. There is no meaning, no cohesion to these seemingly random squiggles. Only by stepping back, by gaining *perspective,* can you see what the picture actually is. Suddenly those marks of blue represent a person, those swirls of green become a tree. By stepping back, by gaining distance, you understand and you recognize.

Similarly, grievers who transcend gain a different perspective on their loss and see it in a new light. These grievers come to recognize the loss as a watershed event in their lives, as a meaningful life turning point. From their higher vantage point, they can see the loss as an integral piece in the puzzle of their lives.

But transcending the loss is not just affirming that the loss is a significant life event. There is one additional, important step. Transcending the loss is about striving to make the experience an ultimately positive and redemptive one, it is about grievers resolved to using their pain in a meaningful and inspirational way. Transcending loss, then, refers to those who have made the best of a terrible situation and have let grief teach them important lessons about life. It refers to those who insist that something tragic can and will lead to something meaningful. These grievers have discovered the gifts that flow from grief.

I want to emphasize that even for those who discover these gifts, who let good flow from bad, even these transcenders still wrestle with the ongoing retriggering pain of Synthesis. They still miss their loved ones desperately. Transcending loss doesn't mean that the pain is any less, or that the pain disappears. Actually, every person with whom I spoke would trade in every "gift," every "gain," every meaningful outcome in a split second if they could only have their beloved back. So transcending loss means choosing a path of transformation in spite of and including the pain.

Transcending the Loss

There is no single way to reach Transcendence or to make the loss meaningful. Surely there are as many different approaches as there are individuals. Furthermore, you don't just have an "aha" moment, an epiphany, and then rest in your state of enlightenment. Transcendence, like Synthesis, is a lifelong, continuous stage with fluid, dynamic properties. The journey continues as Transcendence ebbs and flows, changing over time. What you define as meaningful one year may not be so the next. You are constantly reevaluating, searching anew, redefining. That's what makes Transcendence such a powerful, life-affirming force—it is full of movement and growth.

One of the women I interviewed for this book unwittingly summed up Transcendence for me. She lost her daughter to AIDS almost five years ago. Beverly, who is now sixty-three, has spent many years agonizing over this loss. She went through stages of intense bitterness and anger. She still gets angry. But somehow, in spite of her pain—or maybe because of it—she has reached out to others. She has become active in the AIDS community. She runs support groups, she started a hotline for bereaved mothers, she started the national Mother's March Against AIDS. She is sustained by her faith in God, and she tells me that she is more compassionate than she ever was before. Does she still hurt? Yes. Would she give anything to have her daughter back? Of course. But does her grief make a difference? Is it meaningful? Absolutely. She told me, "There's a hole in my heart that will never be filled up. I laugh now, but I don't laugh full. Whatever I do it's not full, there's always something missing. It'll never be what it was. I have no choice but to accept it. This is it, you know, this is what was handed to me. You're handed a lemon in life, so either you get bitter or you make lemonade."

Time and Transcendence

Turning lemons into lemonade is the essence of Transcendence, and it is the healing goal for this stage. It means taking the materials handed to you and making something meaningful from them, creating something new that never would have existed but for this loss—creating order from chaos, lightness from darkness.

Now, you may be reading this with utter disbelief. You may be thinking to yourself, "No, it's impossible. My pain will never, ever be positive. Nothing good can ever come from this tragedy." And if you're in the stages of Shock, Disorganization, or even the beginning of Reconstruction, then your thoughts are right on target. During these stages it is next to impossible to imagine that good can flow from bad, that something significant can be created from something painful.

Transcendence can only happen *over time*. This is such an important concept that you will find me emphasizing it over and over again. Only over time can you develop a sense of perspective—a sense of detachment, if you will—that can permit this kind of thinking to take root. Only over time can you accept, and maybe even embrace, this piece into the overall puzzle of your life.

It is only natural that in the stages of Shock and Disorganization, your life is consumed and introverted. You turn in and focus on your survival. "I," "me," "mine" are at the center of your universe. As you gradually turn back out into the world, becoming more extroverted in the stage of Reconstruction, your pronouns shift to "you" and "yours." But in Transcendence, it is possible to move into a higher state of connectedness. Your pronouns become "we," ours," and "us." Your fundamental view of the world and yourself shifts as you transcend your grief and reinvest in the living.

If you're not yet ready to accept that gifts can flow from grief, that's okay. Consider this a seed planted in your garden. Just let the seed lie there quietly in the dark, and hopefully, over time, perhaps without your even realizing it or

maybe by working very hard at gardening, the seed will begin to grow, and before you know it, a transcendent flower
will have blossomed right before your eyes.

An Example of the Journey

Perhaps this is sounding rather abstract to you, even es-
oteric. It's always best to get grounded in the particulars, so
here is the story of Patricia, her journey from Shock to Transcendence. Patricia is a forty-one-year-old woman who had
a stillborn child six years ago. At the time, she and her husband, Ron, also had a four-year-old daughter and a two-
year-old son.

I must have known that something was wrong. I'm
usually very large when I'm pregnant and this time I
wasn't. The baby didn't move around enough, I could
feel her moving less and less. But I would ask the midwife if everything was okay, and she would say, "Yes,
just be sure you eat enough." So it was one of my last
visits, I was eight and a half months pregnant, and Ron
was leaving for a business trip. I remember crying before the appointment and saying that I wished Ron
could go with me. I guess I knew something was wrong.
Anyway, I went, and the nurse said, "I can't find a
heartbeat." At that point, I just went into another
world—I was just doing the motions. They had to take
me to the hospital to do the sonogram next, and everybody was just so quiet. What could they say? Finally,
they just told me that my baby was dead. My daughter,
Emily, was dead.

I had to go back home at first to wait for various

calls and permissions at the hospitals for the doctors and the midwives to induce me, or whatever. I was in a fog. I remember Ron coming back from his business trip and I ran out to the car and cried, "Our baby's dead." My midwife, who had birthed my older daughter, told me, "Pat, I need to birth your baby because I also had a stillbirth and I know exactly what you're going through." I just wanted that baby out and fast; I just wanted her out.

Anyway, after she was born—she was only two and a half pounds—my midwife said, "Listen, Pat, you may not want this now, but I'm going to go clean Emily up, and I'm going to take pictures. You can leave them here, but believe me, you will come to rejoice in this baby's birth." She called Emily her little feather. I thought my midwife was absolutely bonkers. I didn't think I'd want any part of this memory or this birth or anything else. But she cleaned her up for us, brought her back, and Emily stayed with us for several hours. Ron just held her and held her. He said he will always remember that she seemed to clutch his finger. There was a part of me that just wanted her out of our room. None of it seemed real. Still, the hardest part was saying goodbye to her and having them take her away.

Six years after the fact, as Patricia told me this story, she began to cry. Actually, virtually everyone I spoke with cried when they told me their story, no matter how long ago the death occurred. That's Synthesis, the ongoing retriggering impact—it's normal; it's natural; the sorrow runs that deep. What Patricia was just describing was the moment of impact and then the stage of Shock. She was at first disbelieving, later numb, and clearly overwhelmed.

Eventually she moved into the delicate balance between Disorganization and Reconstruction, with strong moments of the former and stabilizing moments of the latter.

My son had a birthday two days after, and we were in a dreamworld, carrying on for him to make his birthday a birthday, and getting Emily's ashes and having a memorial for her. It was so unreal. One thing I realized right away was that I wanted to talk about her birth so much, I wanted to tell the story, and I realized that most people didn't want me to. Part of me was resentful for that, because I think it's a need that you have so much. You want them to acknowledge [the loss], you want to be able to talk about it as much as you can.

That summer was such a sad time, but it was more of a sifting in of things getting back to normal, normal day-to-day living. Luckily, Ron grieved very openly and really hard. That was so beneficial because we were then able to unite, instead of breaking apart. He wasn't out there searching for his feelings, they were right in the open. He's not a man who cries openly, but he certainly cried a tremendous amount that summer. I'm so thankful because that really helped us work it through together.

Patricia and Ron did the grief work of Disorganization while continuing to run a household, run their own business, and take care of their two growing children. They let in the emotional pain of Disorganization while gradually rebuilding

their lives in Reconstruction. But what Patricia began to discover is that there was more grief work to do. One year came
and went and still there was more, something unresolved.

> The first year was a kind of sifting, but after that,
> about one year later, I started to get all these stomach
> pains, digestive problems. I was working these long,
> crazy hours, and our business was going belly-up, and
> I was still thinking about Emily. I went to my doctor,
> and he said to me, "Pat, maybe you should go talk to
> somebody." I had never been to a psychologist before.
> I'm not against it, not for it; I had never even thought
> about it. My stomach problems were caused by a lot
> of things, Emily's death being one of them. So I said
> okay, and I did it. I do think that sometimes doors are
> ready to be knocked upon. I found a fellow who was
> just wonderful. So of course, I talked a lot about Emily.
> He opened up meditation to me, and I began to med-
> itate. I began to do things just for myself, to take care
> of me.

Patricia began to see that Emily's death was going to have
to be worked and reworked and then worked again. Even
now, Patricia still feels Emily's presence at times, still feels
her influence in their family. Patricia is seeing the long-range
impact of the loss, the ongoing stage of Synthesis in her life.
She told me:

> You know, after I got your phone call [asking to let
> me interview her for my book], I began to think about
> Emily so much. I had trouble falling asleep for several
> days, and then I had such strange dreams. But that's

okay. Sometimes I'll watch a television program and there will be a woman giving birth, and I'll just break out crying. It's sad; no matter how you look at it, losing a child is sad. I think we as a culture shut sadness out too much. We forget that your heart can be broken— you can be so sad—but you can still be happy. You can be happy at the same time and be sad at the same time.

Sometimes I'll think of her often, depending on what's going on. At times the sadness comes on strong, but then it passes. The feelings come and go, like waves. Sometimes it surprises me that it still gets stirred up, how strong those emotions are embedded in me. It's part of everything.

It's like she's always there—her history, the fact that she existed, that she was there, that's always with us. That's always very real. She's a woven part of our family history. It can never be taken away, it's there, it's tight; in that respect, she's always there.

Patricia is not afraid to accept that there will be retriggerings of this loss. She's not afraid to embrace Emily's memory. She lives her life with the effects of Synthesis. She also dialogues with Emily, both internally and externally.

I feel a spiritual presence in Emily. When I was pregnant again [Pat went on to have another child], I thought, "Oh gosh, I've been meditating, we're a really happy, tight family," and I thought this pregnancy would be a breeze, but forget it, I was a paranoid person. I went out—we have a little bench next to Emily's stone—and I can remember going out there, I must have been five or six months pregnant, and I just broke down in tears and I said, "Oh God, Emily, help me, what is the matter with me?" Then I began to have the most incredibly peaceful feeling. So I went back to see my therapist and I told him about that experience, and he said, "Did Emily answer you?" When I thought about it, it was so clear, I could hear this voice saying, "Pat, just go slowly and open up and just take in all the life that's around you, the trees and the grass, and just slow down and open up. But her voice wasn't a child's voice, it was a very mature, wise, woman's voice. Sometimes I feel that I can really connect with her presence. It was comforting and it brings to light a lot of other questions, like about old souls.

As you listen to Patricia describe Emily's enduring influence and presence in her family's life, you sense that Patricia is receptive to learning from her experience. Although Patricia would not use the word Transcendence—it is my description of her experience—I think you will agree as you listen to her perspective and her lessons learned, that she has reached a higher level of processing.

With the meditation and the reflection in therapy, as soon as I kind of slowed down and opened up, I think a certain spirituality entered my life, a spiritual awareness that wasn't there before. Though I've always believed that there was something greater out there, I could never put my finger on it, and I can't really put my finger on it now. But as I began to slow down and open up, Ron and I began to realize that it was like the worst possible time in our lives—our business was on the brink of bankruptcy, and we had lost a child—and yet we were probably happier than we had ever been in our lives. This all happened about six months after I started therapy and meditating [almost two years after Emily's death]. I think our focus changed. We became very aware that family was the most important thing in our lives and business is just business. Certainly nobody likes to bounce a check or anything else, that was still important, but it was a shift for us. And it was a shift that we both don't think would have happened if Emily had never existed, if Emily hadn't been part of our lives.

In other words, she was the catalyst. She was another door opening up. Emily helped us to refocus. She helped me connect with a spiritual power that . . . I don't understand it, I don't get it. I can't even put it into focus, but boy it's there and it's strong and you can connect in it and to it. I'm in awe of a higher being, a higher power, a connecting light, whatever it may be. It's brought about a lot of questions for me too. Actually, it's brought more questions than answers, but isn't that fun? There are all these things that we don't quite understand but you know that there's meaning, and there's something to it. I don't think I'm going to understand it before I die, but that's okay. I kind of like being at this questioning because it leaves me wide open to discover the wisdom that's in all religions, so wise and wonderful.

Patricia isn't afraid of the questions that grief often brings. She embraces the uncertainty. Part of Transcendence is being open to the process of learning, being open to the process of not knowing. Patricia flows with the process rather than fighting it.

By the grace of God, I was able to open up and grow from this experience. I think it has to do with openness. If you're blessed enough to receive, if you can receive the sadness, you can learn. Let me tell you, about three years before [Emily] was born, I had a dream that really scared the hell out of me. I heard a voice say, "You're dying." I took it to mean maybe I had cancer or something. It made me feel so jittery the next morning, and I thought about it for quite a while. I went and had a checkup. Part of me thinks that it was a message, that my soul was dying. I was so wrapped up in business and work and being busy, and a part of me was trying to wake me up. Emily woke me up.

I'm a different person because I am aware of the importance of not only your family, but of slowing down and connecting with as much as you can, whether it's the neighbors or your extended family. You know when Scrooge, after he's seen the three ghosts, wakes up in the morning and he just realizes life is there and it's there to be had? That's how I feel. There are times when I can walk through New York and feel solitary. There are other times that I can look around and really feel a part of everybody that I see. That is different. That never happened to me before.

I can honestly say that I feel that I was blessed to have had this experience, to have known Emily for even a short time. I feel that I've become so much wiser, I feel that Emily has given me more than anybody else. And she's given my family so much. I feel like she has given me one of the best gifts that anybody could ever receive. How many people go through life in this rush? I still tend to do it sometimes, there's too much cleaning or I get myself in a busy mode, and then your children are a year older. Life is too short. I certainly don't feel blessed that I had a child that died. I'd rather she lived. But I feel blessed in the lessons that I've learned.

Now that is Transcendence! Do you hear how she has grown from this loss? Do you hear how she has connected spiritually and philosophically? Grieving over time is about reaching deeper and deeper levels of acceptance. After Shock, you have to burn through the denial to accept the reality, the shocking truth, that your loved one is dead. Then in Disorganization, you *feel* the reality that your loved one is gone. In Reconstruction, you accept again that he or she is gone and therefore you rebuild physically and psychologically. In Synthesis you accept and accept again, over the years. With Transcendence, your acceptance reaches a new level. Not only do you accept it philosophically and spiritually, you embrace it.

Making Meaning out of Loss

I have said that the way to Transcendence—the way to turning lemons into lemonade, to finding the opportunity in crisis—is to make meaning out of the loss. What an abstract concept, really. What does it mean to find meaning? When I was in high school, I became obsessed with the question "What is the meaning of life?" It's rather an odd question for a teenager to be dwelling on, but I suppose it was part of the normal angst that adolescents must struggle with. I was driven to come to some conclusion, so I set about my search by asking virtually everyone I knew, "What do you think the meaning of life is?"

I did find meaning in that process because what I realized was that everyone answered that question differently. I began to formulate in my adolescent mind that there is no one ultimate meaning. There are many meanings, and each one of them is valid. Furthermore, meaning is fluid and seems to change over time depending on one's circumstances and place in the life cycle.

While there are many avenues for meaning, it seems that finding some meaning—any meaning—is what makes life worth living, and it makes loss worth surviving. Patricia has made meaning out of the loss of her daughter Emily by letting it teach her different priorities in life, by letting it connect her to a spiritual presence.

Dr. Victor Frankl offers us some insights into the human desire for meaning in life. The Austrian psychiatrist and author survived unspeakable atrocities in the Nazi concentration camps during World War II. Additionally, he lost virtually his entire family, including his father, mother, brother, and his wife, in the Holocaust. The horrors of enduring the depraved and despicable conditions of the camps have been well documented now, so it is with particular admiration and wonder that we can analyze Dr. Frankl's subsequent professional contributions. For, rather than succumb to bitterness, isolation, or even mental illness after his release, he went on to formulate the theory of *logotherapy*, or "meaning" therapy.

In *Man's Search for Meaning*, first published in Austria in 1946 and still a best-seller, Dr. Frankl describes his experiences and explains his theory of logotherapy. Essentially, he maintains that we all have a natural drive within us that he calls the "will to meaning." He says that each of us has this desire to find meaning in life, and if it is frustrated or thwarted, then we become depressed, addicted, anxious, and so on. He describes three basic ways to find meaning: in what we give to life, something creative; in what we take from the world, and how we relate to it; and in the stand that we take toward a fate we cannot change, or the attitude we have toward suffering.

Other philosophers say life is about savoring the world, stopping to smell the roses, so to speak. Still others say meaning is made when we grow spiritually, or when we learn lessons out of every experience—positive and negative—here on earth. Some say one must search for larger goals and purposes, something bigger than the self, by committing oneself to causes that will enrich the lives of others and better the world. All of this is Transcendence.

So, mulling this over, I began to look for trends among the grievers that I was working with and interviewing. If they did indeed seem to reach this golden, magical state of Transcendence, if they had that glow of inner serenity despite their sufferings, I wanted to know which paths they took to get there. How did they find meaning in their losses? How did they lift themselves out of their myopic, self-contained pain (that which is initially necessary in grief), and attain a broader, richer vision (that which can only come over time)? What made their losses purposeful and significant?

The SOAR Solution

Patricia found meaning in becoming more spiritually connected, but not everyone finds solace or meaning in spirituality. I listened to others who seemed somehow at peace with their loss but didn't believe in God. They had other ways of making meaning. I asked people about the lessons they had learned, whether or not anything positive can come from something so negative. And as complex and as individual as grief is, I began to notice certain patterns in their responses, certain consistent themes within the experiences of transcendent grievers.

Four common pathways emerged, four roads that made Transcendence possible. I have grouped these four roads into the framework of SOAR—Spirituality, Outreach, Attitude, and Reinvestment—four different roads that lead to a common destination. You can take different modes of transportation on each road, take only one road, or try several different paths. Sometimes the paths merge and blend together, as when your Attitude is also a form of Spirituality, or your Reinvestment is also a type of Outreach. As with the stages of grief, the boundaries are permeable. But whether distinct or overlapping, these four pathways somehow add a quality to grieving that moves it beyond mere acceptance to Transcendence.

I'll be discussing each of the four pathways over the next four chapters to give you a better and more thorough understanding of each road with examples of how people have traveled along them. You will see that both Spirituality and Attitude are internal processes that require inner reflection and processing, while Outreach and Reinvestment are more activity-oriented and directed outward. Each of these pathways is a route toward Transcendence because each encourages transcending the self. With Spirituality you transcend the self to connect with a greater divine spirit. With Outreach, you transcend the self to connect with other people.

With Attitude, you transcend the self to develop a personal philosophy on life and death. And with Reinvestment, you transcend the self to connect with love and with life. The balance of the four is optimal although not necessary. Some people find meaning by traveling down two or more of the paths, whereas others walk only one road.

In the chapters ahead, some people will appear only once or twice as an example of how they traveled one or two of the pathways. But I also met many people who have traveled along all four pathways toward Transcendence. I have chosen one of these individuals—Barbara—to refer to throughout the next four chapters so that you can follow her journey along all four of the SOAR pathways. She will be our SOAR traveler who will exemplify one way of navigating the pathways.

The SOAR solution brings vitality and meaning to life and to grief. If you can become conscious of these options for healing, then you can strive to move in this direction. Transcendent healing is finding spiritual, emotional, and philosophical peace. SOAR can take you there.

In the final analysis, Transcendence cannot be linked to one act, a tangible transaction. Dozens of little acts, thoughts, and beliefs combine, leading to this metamorphosis. It doesn't happen all at once, it happens at last. Remember that you must fully ponder the darkness before you can be transported to light. And know that it takes time to find your way, time to heal, time to transcend. Like a fine red wine that must age and mature before it is ready to be tasted, Transcendence is a process that unfolds over time. It is a subtle and extended journey, but one that ultimately makes life worth living and loss worth surviving.

PART III

The SOAR Solution for Making Loss Meaningful

CHAPTER 6

Spirituality: Religions and Other Roads to the Divine

Suffering is the greatest spiritual teacher.
It is through suffering that one learns
whether God exists.
—AESCHYLUS

A tornado loomed menacingly on the southern horizon, not an uncommon sight in Piedmont, Alabama. Yet the congregation members at the Goshen United Methodist Church were undeterred in attending Palm Sunday services. They went to worship, to praise God, to be together. They did not expect the morning to end in tragedy and destruction. But the tornado swept through the church, leaving twenty people, including six children, dead in its wake. One of those who witnessed this terrible event said, "We are trained from birth not to question God, but why? Why a church? Why those little children? Why? Why? Why?"

One of the children killed was the daughter of the church's minister. A minister, a faithful servant of God, yet her four-year-old daughter was taken. How can one make sense of this? How can one explain? As one observer to the Alabama disaster said, "If that don't shake your faith, nothing will."

For those in Piedmont, Alabama, after the tragic deaths in the tornadoes of 1994, suddenly life just didn't make sense anymore. For most of us, after the death of a loved one, life doesn't make sense anymore. Like an earthquake that shakes the foundations upon which our homes are built, death can shake our foundations of meaning, our foundations of faith. Certainly for some of us, faith holds steadily, but for most of us—at least initially—our faith falters. Ideas we may have held dear crumble, and unexamined truths don't hold up in the harsh glare of interrogation.

Swans, who mate for life, are known to exhibit droopy mourning behavior when their spouse dies. Cheetahs, if their cubs have been devoured by lions, will hover over their dead babies and howl for days on end. But what separates animal mourning from human mourning is that animals lack the capacity to question, to be plagued by the question of "why?" They don't have a faith to shake.

Few of us have the time or energy to contemplate life's mysteries on a daily basis. We're caught up in getting the next promotion, in paying the bills at the end of the month, in planning our vacations, in finding a baby-sitter, in getting to work on time. Who has time to ponder life and death? How many of us regularly question our relationship to the universe or to the Almighty? But then death comes and we are confronted with these issues. Death puts us face to face with the most primitive and basic of existential concepts: we are born, we live, and we die. Death forces us to question the meaning of life, and leaves us with no answers.

My contention is that spirituality is, in the end, a path of great consolation, great strength, and great comfort. For there is a healing force—a spiritual force, an energy greater than the self—that can, if you let it in, mend the broken places in your soul and replenish your depleted waters like an internal reservoir. One's connection to God, then, is ultimately a road to Transcendence. But this path is not such an easy and straightforward one. It is strewn with rocks. What people often don't realize is that it is a natural part of the process for meaning to be lost before meaning can be found. In other words, with grieving, just as you undergo a physical and psychological tearing down and building up, you also experience a parallel process of spiritual destruction and rebirth. If you can withstand the storm, if you can weather the destruction, and even embrace the confusion, it is possible to eventually emerge with a renewed, stronger faith.

Distinguishing Spirituality from Religion

According to a 1992 *Newsweek* poll, 87 percent of Americans state that they believe in God and 78 percent say they pray at least once per week. And yet, many people bristle at the idea of being labeled religious. Others tell me that they're not at all spiritual but then go on to describe their deeply passionate connection with nature or their sense that there is some "higher" force greater than themselves, something else "out there." Or they describe feeling "guided" by some inner force that they cannot name.

My own feeling is that we're essentially spiritual beings. It's human nature to ask "Who am I?" "What am I doing here?" "What's it all about?" "Where am I going?"—

these are spiritual questions. Many of the problems we encounter, I think, are just semantics. But religion and spirituality are vast concepts that mean many different things to many different people. So before we go any further, we should try to define religion and spirituality so that we start from a common understanding.

To begin with, religion and spirituality are not synonyms. Religion refers to our man-made, organized forms of worship—churches, temples, mosques, and the rituals associated with them. These houses of worship offer a formal structure for studying, understanding, and communicating with God. They are also businesses with budgets and fund-raising, governed by human beings, and, as such, subject to the usual human flaws. Because of the inevitable imperfections, many people have turned their backs on organized religion, finding it hypocritical, rigid, inconvenient, and old-fashioned.

Religion, then, is the outward, organized manifestation of spirituality, which is the internal and deeply private relationship to the universe and to the Divine. But again, just as there is often a lot of mistrust about organized religion, there is also a great deal of mistrust around the concept of spirituality. Some eschew the word "spiritual" because to them it seems "flaky" and conjures up images of gurus, crystals, and cults. To others, it is an overused, trendy word of the late '80s and often a lure for scams and frauds. I prefer to think of spirituality as an awareness of and connection to a sacred power that is greater than the self and yet present in each of us.

The kind of spiritual/philosophical journey that grief initiates is common to every type of religion, spirituality, and faith. Being Catholic doesn't exempt you from doubt. There are no Buddhist, Jewish, or Moslem shortcuts. The kind of challenging journey from belief to doubt and back to belief again is truly an interfaith, nondenominational journey. It is a deeply private, individual process of making peace with one's beliefs, one's uncertainties, one's sacred connections. No two of us will do this in precisely the same way. In other words, there is no single way to reach the Divine. Some of us may choose traditional religious routes—Judaism, Christianity, Islam, Buddhism, Hinduism, and others. And others may select nontraditional pathways to the Divine. Although one way may claim to be the only way, I believe that each road is a separate and equally valid route.

The main point is that while we each must choose our own path, we are all as grievers on a similar journey with similar road signs. For some, the journey is brief and relatively simple but for others it is immensely long and complex with many detours and quite a few dead ends. Ultimately we are all searching for avenues of strength, comfort, and peace. Just as the stages of Shock, Disorganization, Reconstruction, Synthesis, and Transcendence apply to the psychological grief process, they also chart a parallel journey of the spirit.

Shock   No Answers Yet, Please

Immediately following the loss of our loved one we ask "Why?" Why did this happen? Why did she have cancer? Why did the car crash? Why now? Why did God allow this to happen? It's important to know that "Why?" at this stage is a rhetorical question. You don't really expect an answer; in fact, you don't want one. "Why?" in the stage of shock is a cry of pain. It's a question that reflects your anguish and confusion, an emotional response to your suffering. Asking

"Why?" in this stage is another way of saying, "I'm in a state of bewilderment and I'm in pain."

As discussed earlier, when you're in shock, you're not in a position to assimilate much of anything. That's why answers to your "Why?" questions at this time are *not helpful*, not now, anyway. Responses like, "It was God's will," or "Your daughter's soul chose to go," or "Your son is in heaven now with Jesus" ask you to deny the truth of your pain. Even if what they say is the philosophy that you will eventually come to believe and accept, in the stage of Shock, you're not ready to hear it.

Dr. William Sloane Coffin, Jr., a minister, writer, and social activist, lost his twenty-four-year-old son in an automobile accident in 1988. Just several weeks after his son's death, he gave a sermon at the Riverside Church in Manhattan entitled "Alex's Death." In it he said:

When a person dies, there are many things that can be said, and there is at least one thing that should never be said. The night after Alex died, I was sitting in the living room of my sister's house outside of Boston, when the front door opened and in came a nice-looking middle-aged woman carrying about eighteen quiches. When she saw me she shook her head, then headed for the kitchen, saying sadly over her shoulder, "I just don't understand the will of God." Instantly I was up and in hot pursuit, swarming all over her. "I'll say you don't, lady!" I said. (I knew the anger would do me good, and the instruction to her was long overdue.) I continued, "Do you think it was the will of God that Alex never fixed that lousy windshield wiper of his, that he was probably driving too fast in such a storm, that he probably had had a couple of 'frosties' too many? Do you think it is God's will that there are no street-lights along that stretch of road, and no guardrail separating the road and Boston Harbor?''

Of course the woman had undoubtedly thought she was offering words of consolation to Dr. Coffin. I'm sure she didn't mean to offend him, nor did she mean to open up a theological debate. But in the stage of Shock, Dr. Coffin found no comfort in her words; he didn't want an explanation for his loss.

A person in shock cannot absorb any explanation. "Why?" is the ultimate question of pain and it doesn't require an answer . . . yet. Even Jesus, in his final moments, cried out, "My God, my God, why hast thou forsaken me?" When a person is in shock, both physically, emotionally, and spirituality, it's the cry of pain that needs to be heard.

Disorganization—Being Lost

After the dust begins to settle, as you start absorbing what has happened, you see that your world has collapsed. Chances are that everything you ever believed in is being questioned and challenged like never before. You cannot possibly be the same or look at life in the same way. You are rudely confronted with a discrepancy between what you expected (that your loved one will be there when you wake up in the morning), what you believed (good things happen to good people), and what is the reality (bad things happen to good people and your loved one is *not* there when you wake up this morning). Once you've been shaken by death and grief, you have a crisis of meaning.

The majority of Americans grew up believing in the Judeo-Christian image of a God who is omnipotent and merciful—the great provider who knows all and controls all. Therefore, if you're going to ask why this death has happened, you're implicitly asking God "Why?" But traditionally, questioning such a force as God is perceived to be a sacrilegious and sinful act that could bring the fury of His wrath down upon you. Thus, for many of us, being angry at God or questioning God is tantamount to heresy. If you do question God, you get to feel guilty and sinful on top of feeling angry and confused. The result is that many people turn their backs completely on God.

The process of questioning one's faith is an extremely complex and personal experience. In *A Grief Observed*, C. S. Lewis beautifully and poetically chronicles his painful struggle with grief and with God after his beloved wife died of cancer. Lewis, a well-known writer and theologian whose faith in God was well grounded and documented, found himself tormented.

Meanwhile, where is God? This is one of the most disquieting symptoms. When you are happy, so happy that you have no sense of needing Him, so happy that you are tempted to feel His claims upon you as an interruption, if you remember yourself and turn to Him with gratitude and praise, you will be—or so it feels—welcomed with open arms. But go to Him when your need is desperate, when all other help is vain, and what do you find? A door slammed in your face, and a sound of bolting and double bolting on the inside. After that, silence. You may as well turn away. The longer you wait, the more emphatic the silence will become. There are no lights in the windows. It might be an empty house. Was it ever inhabited? It seemed so once. And that seeming was as strong as this. What can it mean? Why is He so present a commander in our time of prosperity and so very absent a help in time of trouble? . . . Not that I am (I think) in much danger of ceasing to believe in God. The real danger is of coming to believe such dreadful things about Him. The conclusion I dread is not, "So there's no God after all," but, "So this is what God's really like. Deceive yourself no longer."

Lewis eloquently chronicles his desperate questions and painful doubts. He concludes that his faith was like a "house of cards" that collapsed with one blow. What happens in the book, in his life, is that he gives himself permission to rail against God, to be consumed with anger. He begins to rebuild his house of cards and embarks on a "restoration of faith."

Reconstruction—Being Found

Now it's time to find a philosophy or a belief system to bind your world back together again. Of course, this is easier said than done and will, necessarily, require time for sifting, sorting, questioning, thinking, and exploring. Just as you had to rebuild your daily life after your loved one died, you have to rebuild your internal, philosophical life.

Once C. S. Lewis allowed himself to be angry at God, to

let his faith collapse, he then had the task of putting it back together, and gradually, he starts to make peace with God.

Something quite unexpected has happened. It came this morning early. For various reasons, not in themselves at all mysterious, my heart was lighter than it had been for many weeks. . . . And so, perhaps, with God. I have gradually been coming to feel that the door is no longer shut and bolted. Was it my own frantic need that slammed it in my face?

He concludes his account by referring to God's grand enterprise in orchestrating what happens on earth. By having the courage to express his feelings and doubts, he processed his philosophical and spiritual grief and moved through an experience from faith to doubt to restoration. This spiritual process is normal and typical. However, for many the process becomes thwarted or stuck, so we'll be coming back to this issue in chapter 10.

Finding Light Where Before There Had Been Darkness

Perhaps you're thinking to yourself, "Yes, but I never believed in God in the first place." Maybe you didn't have much of a spiritual view to fall apart, but now is your opportunity to build one. In other words, you can move straight from Shock to Reconstruction. There is no spiritual Disorganization per se because there was no belief system to disorganize. But grief still can initiate a spiritual quest because it brings to light questions and answers that might not have been considered otherwise.

Once I heard a griever in a bereavement support group

talk about how after his wife died, he also began to get in touch with a spiritual connection that he had never before experienced. He said discovering that connection in life was "as if I had been living my whole life thinking there were only AM channels and suddenly discovering that there are FM channels too. It has opened up an entire new world to me, a new frequency."

Patricia, too, described having a similar experience after Emily's stillbirth, of discovering a spiritual life that she hadn't had before. Through meditation, through therapy, through sensing Emily's presence and influence, she found a connection to the Divine. "As soon as I kind of slowed down and opened up, I think a certain spirituality entered my life, a spiritual awareness that wasn't there before." She said she always believed that "something" was out there, but she never felt in touch with it, never could grasp it. Now, since Emily's death—*because of* Emily's death—she does.

Often people tell me that they had some vague understanding of a God, but that they had essentially turned their backs on the religions of their childhoods and had never bothered to figure out what they really believed. Their lives became filled with the daily minutiae of living and their spiritual lives were squarely placed on the back burner. But with the deaths of their loved ones, and over time, they were forced by the grief journey onto a spiritual journey. What they found there has led them to Transcendence.

Spirituality as a Pathway to Transcendence

Certainly religion and spirituality can be a balm right from the beginning of one's journey with grief. Many people told me that even in the stages of Shock and Disorganization they prayed for strength, they were consoled by their minister or rabbi, they read religious literature and found peace. Certainly one's relationship with God can be a comfort, a tremendous coping resource, throughout every stage of grieving. But as a pathway to Transcendence, something different occurs. In Transcendence, one's spiritual relationship is nourished, changed, strengthened, enriched *as a result of your loss*. In other words, the experience of loss deepens your relationship with the Divine in a way that didn't exist before and that might not ever have existed were it not for this experience.

Remember that none of us has all the answers. We must learn from one another on the journey. Here are some stories of how others have traveled the pathway of Spirituality and have found meaning, consolation, and Transcendence there. Perhaps one of their stories will ring true for you or even point you in the direction of your own spiritual peace.

BARBARA'S STORY—RETURNING TO HER ROOTS

Barbara is our SOAR traveler who we will be following through the next several chapters. She is a fifty-year-old woman whose younger brother, Bobby, died of AIDS in 1989 at the age of thirty-one. Barbara was twelve years older than her brother. When they were younger, they were extremely close. Barbara says, "He was my adored baby brother. He was just the cutest, dearest little boy. I adored him and took care of him. He, in fact, thought of me as a second mother."

As the years went by, Bobby became wilder and more adventuresome. He was a free spirit that flew in the face of the staid, WASPy New England family that he found himself in. "Even as a little boy, he took up so much space; he whirled; he had so much energy. He was so full of life. Bobby was wonderfully, wonderfully opposite. He was open, but we as a family were not. I often think it's almost as though he was programmed from the start to have a short, fast life. He lived at four times the speed of any of the rest of us."

By senior year in high school, Bobby announced that he was gay and that he was leaving to spend the summer with his male lover. The family was shocked and thought this was a stage that he would somehow "outgrow."

Bobby's wild, good-time ways led him into a life of drugs, parties, and promiscuity. He and Barbara grew further and further apart. "I was a very different person then. Instead of loving him in spite of it, or working with it, I just thought, 'I really don't like this. I don't like being around drunks, I don't like being around drugs. Why doesn't my brother just sit down and have a normal, quiet conversation with me?' That's how it was. He lived his wild New Orleans life and I lived my New York life. We talked every once in a while but we definitely weren't close."

Several months before Bobby died, Barbara was contacted by Bobby's lover about his illness, and the lines of communication were opened again. "Through those months, Bobby and I were on the phone with each other a lot. He became deeper and deeper and more and more honest." Barbara didn't realize just how sick Bobby was then, so several months later when she got the phone call that he had died, she was shocked.

I remember horrible days. Grief for me was completely physical. I was freezing cold all the time. I could never get warm. I took to my bed. I didn't see people.

I followed wherever grief took me and I didn't resist it. I was like a wounded dog. I retreated, and that's how I healed.

I didn't know how to grieve, few of us do; in this culture we just don't. But I did it exactly as I needed to do it. That included being so angry, so angry at God. I would go to John [her minister] in tears and say, "How can the world be so mean?" My first questions were very simplistic; it was very much the "It's no fair," as though this were a child's game and fairness had anything to do with anything. Then the anger got much bigger and was directed at God, and I was full of guilt. I yelled at God out loud. I remember I went to a monastery on the Hudson just to get away from everything for a while, for a long weekend, and I was walking in the fields, and at one point I just raised up my fist [to God] and I shouted, "Why don't you come out and fight like a man?"

So I was reading a book by C. S. Lewis called *A Grief Observed*, an extraordinary book, and I guess this was God coming out and fighting like a man, because suddenly I read the thing that made sense to me after all this searching. [Lewis] said something like, "I think many of the questions we ask God are like nonsense questions. Our saying 'why?' is like saying 'Is orange square?' or 'Is yellow round?' " Suddenly it made sense to me. I was having a childlike idea of God. My insisting that God answer as though I were calling him on the phone really revealed to me that I thought I could understand what God was. And what was riveting about that little passage was that I realized anything I make up is going to be based on a human concept, and whatever God is, it's not human.

So, after Barbara retreated, after she felt her feelings, after she allowed herself to be angry at God, and after she was open to hearing answers, she started to heal. A big part of her healing was a spiritual healing.

There has been a real change for me. I used to be almost embarrassed to use the word God. But now, I have no question that God—whatever, however we think of God—is absolutely working in my life. I feel that since Bobby died I have been on a spiritual express train, not just a path, but an express train. That's just one of many things that has happened that seems to be drawing me back to the person I am.

As a little girl, I was deeply, deeply religious. We lived in the country and I was always full of reverence for the nature all around me. I would get down on my knees and thank God for the beauty of it all. I remember wanting to grow up to be saintly, and I used to really work on being nice. Something about Bobby's death opened me in a way that made it possible for me to come home again.

Barbara said that even before Bobby died, she had gone in search of a church because she realized that for many, many years she was suffering from a kind of "homesickness," a spiritual yearning. She found a Unitarian church, a liberal religious tradition, that brought her comfort and peace. After Bobby's death, however, and after some internal political problems in this particular congregation, she left this church to go on a personal spiritual odyssey.

Barbara began her journey first by studying Eastern religions in depth, particularly Buddhism and Hinduism. She traveled to Germany twice to be with an Indian saint. As a result of studying these religions, she was led, interestingly, right back to her Christian roots.

I've always found being Christian a little bit . . . even saying it now I find it a little bit embarrassing. It's not something I've been comfortable with. I always thought that my California cousins, who were born-again Christians, were just really weird, as we thought Bobby was weird. Bobby had become a Jesus "freak" when he was a teenager, which in our family was probably worse than being gay. We made terrible fun of him. But anyway, I needed to connect to something larger. The studies of Eastern religions brought me around to an understanding of Jesus in a way that I can only say has been a gift from somewhere.

Then later, I had this extraordinary experience. I had felt for years, since Bobby died, a real need to go to Chartres. I studied it and read about it, and just felt I had to get there. I kept thinking there's going to be some answers for me in Chartres. I don't know, I just felt drawn to it. But there was never a time to go. Well, suddenly I had an assignment to go to Paris, and I thought, perfect, my way is paid, I'll take a day and I'll go. The night before I went, I met a woman from California and we had dinner together that night. When I told her what I was doing the next day, she said, "Instead of taking the train, why don't you let me drive you to Chartres?" So, in the car, she begins to talk about her faith, which was a burning, burning deep faith. I went into Chartres and whatever it was that I was expecting to happen, didn't happen. I kept thinking the answer's here, I know the answer's here. I came back and she was waiting for me and I got into the car and she said, very quietly, "You know, all you need to do is . . ."—and the words sound so weird, if I had heard these words outside of this context, I would have thought, "oh, too weird"—but she said, "all you have to do is invite Jesus into your heart." I had felt the answer was going to be at Chartres, and maybe the answer came from this woman. And she was the sort of woman that I would listen to. She was really smart, she was a tough businesswoman, there was nothing weird about her. I could respect her. And from her I could hear it.

Barbara has a totally different understanding of Christianity now. She has gone back to attend a Protestant church, which has brought its own brand of challenges and obstacles. Barbara says, "I have a real problem with organized religion, and I don't want to put all my needs and all my hopes in an institution because I do think—and I can say this now without bitterness—I think institutions, since they are human, are basically corruptible. And chances are they're going to corrupt." But Barbara still attends; she just knows that she needs to nourish her own private spiritual relationship with God and with Jesus.

Barbara's story is of a woman on a journey who, because of her brother's death, found a spiritual life that was strengthened, enriched, and broadened. For her, that meant reclaiming her Christian heritage.

HAROLD'S STORY—INCORPORATING NEW IDEAS

For many, it is not a matter of reconnecting to a past tradition or belief, it's a matter of expanding a current set of ideas so that one's frame of meaning doesn't crack. It means rethinking beliefs, incorporating new ones, and allowing old ideas to be discarded while new ones take their place.

Harold Kushner is a rabbi, a writer, and a parent . . . a bereaved parent. His son Aaron died in 1977, just two days after his fourteenth birthday. When he was eight months old, Aaron stopped gaining weight. When he was one year old, he started losing his hair. When Aaron was just three years old, on the day that the Kushners' second child, Ariel, was born, the doctors visited the family in the hospital to inform them that Aaron had a rare condition called progeria, or "rapid aging." The prognosis was grim as the doctor described that Aaron's growth would be stunted, that he would age like an old man while still a child, and that he would most likely die in his early teens.

Harold and his wife were stunned. How could they make sense of this? Harold was a young rabbi at the time and he remembers thinking, "How could this be happening to my family? If God existed, if He was minimally fair, let alone loving and forgiving, how could He do this to me?" In his wonderfully wise and compassionate best-selling book, *When Bad Things Happen to Good People*, Harold writes, "Like most people, my wife and I had grown up with an image of God as an all-wise, all-powerful parent figure who would treat us as our earthly parents did, or even better. If we were obedient and deserving, He would reward us. If we got out of line, He would discipline us, reluctantly but firmly. He would protect us from being hurt or from hurting ourselves, and would see to it that we got what we deserved in life."

In this book Harold chronicles his spiritual journey: how his frame of meaning cracked when his beliefs no longer made sense; how he discarded these previously cherished ideas and searched for new ones; how he ultimately reconstructed his faith and his concept of God.

What happened to Harold after this tragic death is that his theology changed, his beliefs about how the world operated changed, and his relationship with God changed. Harold came to believe that God is not responsible for everything that happens in our world—there are other factors, such as biology, laws of nature, free will. These things explain why bad things happen. Harold told me:

The hard part was abandoning the early, simple faith and essentially having a vacuum there while I was ostensibly functioning as a rabbi and a religious leader for a congregation. I read everything I could find. The key—it's a very important document in my life—was a sermon that Archibald McLeash gave in a church in Connecticut about a play he had written. He doesn't say it quite as explicitly as I ended up saying it, but there it was, the answer I was looking for, that essentially God is not responsible for everything that happens in the world. And God suffers along with us and cries along with us. At that point, everything fell into place. I could be angry at the disease and angry at the bad luck, but I didn't have to be angry at God. The anger didn't have to be a barrier between me and God.

I asked Harold how he, as a rabbi, counsels other grievers.

I try to get people to see God, not as the source of the illness, the accident, the tragedy, but as the source of their own resilience. The only way you can go through this is not by relying only on your own strength, which you intuitively sense is inadequate, but [by knowing] that God is with you in this. This is what really was crucial for me when we found out how sick our son was. If I thought that for whatever obscure, complicated, ultimate reason God was doing this, I don't think I could have tolerated that. But to know that God was on my side, I could continue to turn to him for strength because he wasn't the perpetrator.

I felt something which I [now understand] to be God's guidance. The capacity to love a physically handicapped, terminally ill child, the capacity to survive his death, to survive his death with my faith and my capacity to believe in life intact, to dedicate myself to helping others survive their losses, I see this as the intervention of God in my life. I didn't understand it at the time, but I see it in the way my son lived. That this child who was in constant physical and psychological pain could be such a happy, caring, compassionate child. He couldn't have simply done that on his own, there had to be an influx of divine impulse.

Harold was able to reconnect with his God. He was able to find a deeper, more enriched relationship to the Divine and to his religion. Harold knows that his faith has gotten stronger as a result of this loss. He says:

Faith worked for me in about the most demanding situation I can think of. And because I've seen it work for others, I know it works. I would never say that God did this to bring about a good end. What I can say is that this horrible, painful thing happened because of biology and genetics and there was nothing anybody could do about it. But once it was fated to happen, God showed me how I could take this tragedy and redeem it from simply being a medical statistic and turn it into something redemptive.

Rabbi Kushner's book shares his spiritual journey and enrichment with millions of people. He transcended the loss by making it meaningful, by touching so many lives, and by helping so many people.

Finding a Spiritual Path

Harold Kushner, as a rabbi, is obviously a supporter of organized religion. He told me that he thinks religion is indispensable to the grieving process. "It's replenishment and it's community and . . . people use ritual to control chaos. Death represents the eruption of chaos into our lives. What you need at that time is community. You need people and rituals around you to tell you what to do, to ward off chaos."

The Jewish faith does indeed have many beautiful rituals related to grief. One is "sitting Shiva," a tradition of honoring the deceased and their survivors for seven days. Another is the Kaddish, or mourners' prayer, which is recited during synagogue services. In the Christian tradition there is the wake and the post-funeral reception. Some religions have many rituals related to grief, others just a few. But perhaps one of the strongest supports that organized religion can offer during times of grief is a solid community of caring people, a repository of support and concern. One griever, after the deaths of two of her sons, sought organized religion. "I realized that I needed people and that I needed a community. I couldn't live in isolation. For me, I'm not sure if faith exists in a vacuum. I think it's very much being a part of a larger group. The support that the congregation and ministers give is invaluable."

Rachel was twenty-six when her mother died. Now her stepmother is dying from the same disease that claimed her mother's life—cancer. Rachel is no stranger to loss; at the age of three she lost a newborn sibling, and at the age of twelve her maternal grandmother died. Each of these deaths was traumatic and distressing, creating a climate of loss and sadness in her life.

Although raised in the Jewish tradition, Rachel never had a firm religious grounding. Her father was a Polish Jew, her mother an agnostic. She said, "To me, the Jewish attitude toward death and dying is really harsh. The way I learned it, Jewish tradition is based on the here and now, sort of materialistic in that sense. So there isn't this feeling of flow and eternity and all of that, at all. It's like you have to hang on with every gasp to life. Death is the enemy to be staved off at all costs."

Several years after her mother's death, she met a Catholic nun who had a profound influence on her spiritual development. This nun was a medical missionary for fifteen years and taught Rachel that death was a natural phenomenon and that death was a part of life. "She taught me that it wasn't necessary to cling to every shred of life, there was existence beyond this life. She really believed that death was not something to be feared, that it was okay. I had never heard that before. It was just what I was looking for. It was the missing piece for me."

It was at this point that Rachel truly began to reflect on what these deaths and losses had meant to her. And it was also at this point that Rachel began her spiritual pilgrimage in earnest.

> I began reading about reincarnation, afterlives, death and dying, astrology, Buddhism. My whole belief system was beginning to change and evolve at that point. I went on this voyage in response to my pain and I've come to a place of acceptance of my destiny. I began to see that this incarnation, or this life that I'm living, has a lot to do with recognizing that emotional loss of various kinds is a stepping-stone to a certain kind of liberation and freedom.

Rachel now identifies herself as a Buddhist and responds to the Buddhist doctrine of detachment, or acceptance of loss. Detachment is a concept that was made clear to me once when I watched a group of Buddhist monks painstakingly making a painting out of sand. The design was incredibly intricate and detailed and took the monks nearly three weeks to complete. After they finished their masterpiece they carefully took it to the edge of the Hudson River, where they flung it into the water. The message was one of detachment. Rachel concludes,

> I really don't believe that there's anything I could lose that would devastate me. First of all, I don't think that anything is really ever lost. It's all still with us

everywhere. I feel much more open and free now and much less frightened. I am an aspect of God, or Buddha, all of us are; we're all reflections of that universal energy.

Rachel embraces the spiritual path that she discovered as a result of the losses and deaths in her life.

Prayer

One way that Spirituality manifests itself is in the communication process of prayer, communicating with God/ Goddess/Jesus/Buddha/Allah/Higher Power/Great Spirit/ Mother Nature. Many people told me that since the loss of their loved one they have prayed with an intensity, a regularity, a passion that they had never experienced before.

Prayer is a big part of Cindy's spiritual life. Cindy is a forty-year-old woman who is no stranger to loss and tragedy. She was fourteen when her father committed suicide by shooting himself with a gun. Then in 1983, at the young age of thirty-two, Cindy was diagnosed with breast cancer. A mastectomy was successfully executed, and Cindy was given a clean bill of health. Then, in 1989, Cindy's mother unexpectedly died of breast cancer. In 1991, doctors found another lump in Cindy's remaining breast and she has had to fight the cancer again. Cindy explains,

I'm a very spiritual person but I don't go to church or anything like that. I'm sort of turned off by organized religions. I've been on a spiritual journey for the past eight years. That's one thing that cancer did; it made me feel a lot closer to God, and I embarked on this spiritual journey. I do a lot of reading and thinking; I spend about forty-five minutes every day praying. I feel like I have this close, intense relationship with God.

My spiritual life is the only thing that gets me through, otherwise I think I would have been dead years ago without it, just from despair if nothing else. All you have to do is talk to Him and He'll answer. You don't even have to believe, just talk to Him and He will answer. I know that He answers prayers. Just say, "Help me understand why this had to happen." The way God communicates is very subtle.

There are traditional religious prayers—such as the Lord's Prayer, the Kaddish, the Psalms, the Bhagavad-Gita—and there are private, personal prayers. As people told me of their own prayers, I realized that most of their prayers were for strength or guidance, not for specific actions. So rather than praying, "Please, God, don't let her die," or "Please bring her back," they prayed, "Help me through this" or "Lord, give me strength and help me understand." One griever whose husband committed suicide, leaving her with two small children, prayed, "If you can't do anything else for me, at least give me strength to go on and get these kids grown and give them a decent lifestyle." In the words of Ethel Barrymore, the great American actress, "When life knocks you to your knees—well, that's the best position in which to pray, isn't it?"

And people don't just pray to a higher spirit. Many people pray to their loved ones as well, sustained by the belief that their loved ones are in heaven (or some other spirit world) watching down on them. Some grievers described feeling that their loved one is like a guardian angel guiding and protecting them. A prayer to a deceased loved one is just another example of the ongoing Connection and internal Dialogue that are two components of the lifelong stage of Synthesis. This relationship is forever.

But prayers to the deceased are not just about keeping the attachment alive in this life; they're also about anticipating a reunion in the next life. Over and over again I hear grievers say they are comforted and nourished by the idea of a heavenly reunion. One griever said, "It comforts me to think that my relatives are all together. Sometimes I go to the cemetery and talk to them all up there. I know we'll all be together again one day." One widow told me, "I keep saying that he's waiting for me . . . so I know when I die, I'll be with him again. I don't have any fear of death." Belief in a celestial reunion of spirits takes the sting out of our own mortality.

Connecting with Nature

There are so many ways of experiencing the Divine, of developing a relationship with it, of cultivating a spiritual life. Connecting to a higher power has to do with transcending the self and connecting to a force larger than the self, but it isn't necessary to use the word God. One's relationship with nature may be just as spiritual.

Anna is a woman who lost her husband to cancer ten years ago, after they had been married for sixteen years. They had three children together. She has grieved. She has remarried. She is extremely active in her church community and is a lay leader in her congregation. She told me about her faith.

In my preaching, I say that I feel that belief in God is the wrong question. God is not a matter of belief or not belief. The question is do you *experience* God. If you ask me if I experience the creative force, I would say yes. But I would also put that in more natural terms. I perceive myself to be irrevocably linked to the totality of the universe. But I don't believe in God. I experience the universe. Belief is irrelevant to me. I *experience* that linkage, and I tend to experience it in a natural setting.

There's a book called *The Zen of Walking*, or something like that, by Alan Watts, about what you experience when you're walking. When I'm out walking five, six, seven miles, particularly in a natural setting, I feel connected to all the walkers and all of nature. That cuts through time. I feel that we are all of equal spirits.

Another woman heavily influenced by nature, Leslie, suffered two miscarriages within nine months of each other. Leslie studied with a Native American tribe in New Mexico and was profoundly affected by their teachings. As she talked about her faith, she emphasized her connection to the earth, seeing the cycles of life in nature, the death and the rebirth in the seasons. She said, "Nature makes me feel connected to a much, much greater thing than I. It's humbling. I'm an infinitesimal cog in the wheel. I'm a flicker, a part of one great sun. The total me is a part of the greater whole. We're all connected." As a result of Leslie's losses, she has become more connected to a philosophy that reveres nature.

The Power of a Spiritual Connection

A process of doubt and despair and anger at God is typical when you are experiencing grief. If you give in to, rather than fight the flow of the process, if you are open to the search, and if you are receptive to divine inspiration, it is possible to arrive at a more profound relationship with the Divine.

Every year at St. Vincent's Hospital, where I lead bereavement groups, we hold an annual memorial service for those who have died within the past year. In the closing prayer, we say, "You are a God who never promised joy without pain, or sun without rain, or roses without thorns. But you promised to be with us in our struggles, to give light in times of darkness."

Your loss can lead to an authentic connection with God, perhaps a connection that is richer and deeper than any that existed before. There is no doubt that Spirituality can ultimately become a pathway of meditative contemplation, religious devotion, and divine inspiration. And within this divinity, there is meaning.

The people discussed in this chapter made their losses meaningful by allowing their losses to become catalysts for arriving at these profound places in the heart where they could experience the Divine in unprecedented ways. That is what takes them to Transcendence, a process that unfolds over time and shines a pathway from darkness to light.

CHAPTER 7

Outreach: Helping Others

———

We make a living by what we get,
we make a life by what we give.
—WINSTON CHURCHILL

"It is better to give than to receive." Who hasn't heard this when we were growing up? And yet how many of us thought, "Yeah, yeah, but give me my presents?" Children are an amazing study in pure human emotions. They haven't been taught yet by our society how to censor and repress. They haven't been formed into our cultural molds.

As such, they are an interesting blend of conflicts and contradictions. On the one hand, they are incredibly selfish, self-serving, and self-centered. "Give me! Mine, mine, mine! I come first." They seem to embody the central tenets of Darwinism—survival of the fittest. From an evolutionary perspective, you can see the innate drive to protect the self, to watch out for your own interests, to put yourself and your needs above all others'. But on the other hand, at times, children can be so thoughtful, so giving, so shockingly selfless that it takes your breath away. I once heard a three-year-old child comforting her tearful friend, "No worry, I take care of you. It's okay." And with that she gave her friend a big bear hug.

Children reflect to us our opposing internal forces, our dual natures: we are supremely selfish and we are graciously giving.

The United States of America, as the largest and greatest democracy ever in history, was founded philosophically on respecting the rights of the individual. What this has amounted to in our society is that self-indulgence abounds. The "me" generation continues to promote the glory of oneself. Media reflects this narcissistic obsession. I was once struck by the advertising campaign of a potato chip company touting the tag line, "Grab your own bag." It's a dog-eat-dog world out there—why share?

This very glorification of the selfish self is exactly what is needed in the initial stages of bereavement. During the stages of Shock, Disorganization, and even the beginning of Reconstruction, it is crucial that you focus on the self. In these stages your grief demands a selfishness, an internal focus, in order to heal. You are in no position to give of the self since your self, your world, has been shattered. Even if you have other people in your life depending on you emotionally and financially, your giving is on the most minimal level possible. Your resources are depleted and there's not much left to go around.

But once you emerge through Disorganization, once you pass through Reconstruction, and once you settle into the reality of Synthesis, something must shift. You have two choices. You can continue to focus in and develop an insular perspective on life, and thereby remain stuck in your grief and self-pity. Or you can travel toward Transcendence. In the last chapter, we talked about pathways of spirituality or transcending the self to connect with a divine power. The next pathway is about transcending the self to connect with other people, a pathway of outward, not inward, focus, the pathway of Outreach.

Outreach is a practical, activity-directed, task-focused pathway. It means giving service, doing volunteer work, helping other people. It means reaching out to others who suffer; it means having your actions reflect compassion and tolerance. It means, for a moment, putting someone else's needs above your own.

Now, I'm not suggesting that you do this obsessively, to the detriment or even exclusion of your own needs. We have all heard of compulsive caretakers who always focus on others and never themselves. Or codependents (an overused word in recent years, I know) who direct all of their attention on someone else (the dependent) rather than sticking up for themselves. No, Outreach as a road to Transcendence means taking care of yourself first, but then using your pain, your loss, your sorrow as fuel for helping other people, for making a difference in someone else's life.

Michael is a thirty-five-year-old man whose brother was killed during a violent crime. Well over ten years later, Michael is still deeply affected by his brother's death. Michael has gone through a lot in mourning his brother, Alex, emotionally and spiritually. He nicely summarizes Outreach.

Being involved in change, being involved in trying to better things—that's my vocation now. It's important in healing too. It gets the attention off of yourself. The grief still exists, but you can turn it around. You can make it into something that helps other people with what you know and what you've learned.

One of the things I would definitely recommend to anybody who is going through any kind of loss is, as soon as they're strong enough, to be involved in helping other people who have been through the same thing. This is kind of a gross analogy, but it's the best one I can think of: It's like you sort of have this emotional bladder that must be relieved. If you're constantly in a state of helping other people with their healing, you're flushing yourself out. It's a purifying thing. There are certain toxins in your body and you work out and perspire them away, you keep some kind of flow going. It's the reason I'm still in one piece—it really works. That's my recipe—get it out and help other people in ways that you can.

As Michael suggests, Outreach detoxifies your system. Ironically, reaching out and giving to others is a selfish act. Why? Because it benefits the giver as much as, if not more than, the receiver. In other words, you give because it makes you feel good; it nourishes your soul; it eases your grief; it bolsters your self-esteem; it brings you closer to God; it fulfills you; it heals you; it provides you with meaning.

It is difficult to imagine "pure" altruism. Consciously or otherwise, you benefit from being altruistic and that is part of the motivation to do the good in the first place. Rabbi Kushner addressed this issue with me when I asked him about making meaning and giving.

First of all, I think for everybody, whether you're recuperating from a loss or not, for anybody to be concentrated on yourself instead of giving to other people is a recipe for unhappiness and loneliness. I think anybody who's concerned mostly with taking his or her own temperature is not a very happy person.

With giving to others, the real insight is that that's the ultimate self-interest. You can't tell people to be too noble, that everybody should be Mother Teresa. But when you understand that this is the *cure*, this is the way to heal, and this is the way you recover your own sense of potency, that this is something you have to do for yourself, then I'm not asking you to be noble and self-sacrificing. I'm asking you to do what you need to do to heal and feel good about yourself.

Harold tells us that Outreach is part of the recipe for deep healing. It's a paradoxical prescription, but the bottom line is that if you help others, you will help yourself. As Sir James Barrie, a British philosopher, says, "Those who bring sunshine to others cannot keep it from themselves."

Helping Other Grievers

Let's look at a specific example of Outreach: helping other grievers. Because of the loss that you have sustained, you understand deep pain, sorrow, doubt, and conflict in a way that many people do not. You have been exposed to darkness, and you can use this knowledge to make you an unusually sensitive and compassionate consoler. When you hear of someone who has a loss, call, write, visit, or just listen.

Rabbi Harold Kushner explained,

As you listen to their story of grief, you begin to understand that you're qualified to help in a way that 99 percent of people cannot. The sense of helplessness starts to lift. When you realize that you can help people in a way that the average person can't *because* of your experience, you have the option of turning this into something good, something redemptive, something helpful. You can do it just by knowing, saying the right things.

A number of the grievers I met couldn't find support groups in their area that addressed their needs. So what did they do? They started their own groups, both to help themselves and to reach out to help other grievers. In church basements and community rooms all around the country, self-help grief groups are springing up, started by other grievers out of their own pain and out of their own need for Outreach. Barbara, our SOAR traveler whose brother died of AIDS seven years ago, is one of those grievers. Let's look at some of the many ways that she uses Outreach in her healing process.

Barbara's Story

As a result of her beautiful book *Landscape Without Gravity* (which I'll be discussing in more detail in chapter 9), Barbara received volumes of mail from siblings saying that they needed a place to connect with other bereaved siblings.

I thought in grief groups, in general grief groups, those who had lost siblings took a backseat to others, as though grief were stratified, as though there's a kind of grief that's worse than another kind of grief. So I thought what I need to do is to get [grieving siblings] alone so that they don't fall into this sense that they have to be quiet and not complain.

So Barbara started her first sibling grief group in New York City, and called it "Sisters." The group is comprised of primarily women, but once in a while she does find a man who lost a sibling and wants to join with the Sisters. The groups run for six weeks, and many continue on an informal basis after that. Barbara describes their meetings this way:

What I've noticed in every group, the first thing that happens, before they open their mouths, they get in that room, they look around at each other and there's this sigh of relief. They're with each other. I want to give these people a chance to be completely open about their grieving and receive support.

An important part of the work that Barbara does with the Sisters is that she encourages them on a path of Outreach as well.

I absolutely believe, and I tell all the Sisters this, that at a certain point, whenever you're ready—and this is different for everybody, and I don't ever boss them around because I think there's nothing worse than these grief bosses who say, "You've had this much time now, it's time to get on with your life"—but I do tell them that probably the final healing, a deeply important force for healing, is helping others. Preferably you go right back to the wound, but this time you go back as a healer rather than a victim. And you will be healed; there is no question in my mind that you will be healed. Somebody whose sister died of leukemia, I sent to a place that dealt with that. Somebody whose brother died from AIDS, I sent to GMHC. It doesn't have to be the same, but I think it helps.

Part of it is mysterious, there's so much about healing that I don't know. But I do think that there's something important about going as a healer, going back where you were wounded, going back to the source of the wound but going as a healer, seeing yourself, making that turn from victim to healer. I also encourage them to reach out to anybody who has suffered a loss, because they understand what it's like, and that's also important for their own healing.

Barbara practices what she preaches as well. Since her brother's death, she has become active in the gay community, helping people suffering with AIDS. She started volunteering at a place called Friends in Deed, an organization dedicated to helping people with AIDS. She began to cook for people with AIDS, she began to visit people dying from AIDS. She became involved in the community.

Reaching out to other people who are suffering helps immeasurably. Possibly it's because you're doing for someone else, but it's not that therefore your mind isn't on your own pain. That's true in other areas of life, like if you're feeling depressed nothing helps more than to be distracted. But this is very different; it isn't a distraction; this is something much more powerful.

Any sort of service that we do always benefits us so much more than the person that we're reaching out to. It's truly an example of "it's more blessed to give than receive," which I always thought was "oh yeah, right." Now I understand it.

Barbara is very clear that in her giving, she is a receiver. Through her giving, she has reached a new stage of healing, a level of Transcendence.

For the young men I fed at Friends in Deed, yes, I gave them a good meal and then they were grateful and they went on about their days. But I carry each one of them in my heart. Their gift to me was more blessed because then I take it through life.

And I feel very much in the Sisters groups that there's some wonderful force at work. I know on the simplest level, before I start each one, I really don't want to do it. It's always daunting; it always makes me afraid. I always think I'm not up for it, and it also is terribly time-consuming and I resent having to take time away from my writing. But I get in there with each new group, I sit down, I look at them, they start telling their stories, and I love them. I absolutely love them. And they are and they do become my sisters and my brothers.

Transcending the Self

No one ever said that Outreach was easy. Barbara notes that it may become emotionally draining or overly time-consuming. But she also realizes the healing value of Outreach and so she is able to transcend the self. If you are too immersed in your own needs, then there is no energy to offer to others. So before you are in a position to give, you must transcend the self. Norman Lear, the television producer and director responsible for the hit TV series "All in the Family" (among others), was interviewed in a religious magazine called *The World* in 1992 and talked about his spiritual quest. He essentially describes transcendence of the self.

LEAR: I would describe it [his spiritual quest] as a greater sense of wholeness, and I would say the road to it is, in the words of St. Francis, "By so forgetting, one finds. By dying, one enters eternal life." I don't think St. Francis meant just dying in the literal sense. I think he also meant that by dying in the self and becoming "self-less" one enters the wholeness of Being.

INTERVIEWER: But how does someone like Norman Lear lose himself?

LEAR: It's in the tiny moments. I've got a three-and-a-half-year-old son—that's where I'd like to lose myself. Or in this conversation: losing the sense of self in the moment. Joseph Campbell said, "Most people are not seeking a religious experience; they're seeking the experience of living." Well, the experience of living, I'm convinced, is getting one's self out of the way. That's when you really live—when you are connected to the whole.

Norman Lear nicely summarizes how enriching and ultimately fulfilling it is to transcend the self. He goes on to caution that while one can strive toward this goal, it only happens some of the time. After all, there are many times when you do need to focus on the self. Nevertheless, when you manage to transcend the self, you connect to a greater whole, and from this vantage point—like being at the top of the Empire State Building—it's possible to see things that you never saw before.

Lear also points out that for him, self-transcendence is part of his spiritual development. He refers to St. Francis of Assisi, whose often-quoted prayer is really a prayer about Transcendence, about shedding the self.

> Lord, make me an instrument of Thy peace.
> Where there is hatred, let me sow love.
> Where there is injury, pardon.
> Where there is doubt, faith.
> Where there is despair, hope.
> Where there is sadness, joy.
>
> O divine Master,
> grant that I may not so much seek to be consoled, as to
>   console;
> to be understood, as to understand;
> to be Loved, as to love;
> for it is in giving that we receive,
> it is in pardoning that we are pardoned,
> and it is in dying that we are born to eternal Life.

As this prayer indicates, in order to help others you must slough off the self, putting your needs secondary. This prayer also reflects the spiritual nature of Outreach. At this point Outreach and Spirituality as pathways to Transcendence can begin to overlap.

Outreach and Spirituality

The pathways of Outreach and Spirituality can intertwine. Henry David Thoreau wrote:

> *If I can put one touch*
> *of a rosy sunset into the*
> *life of any man or woman,*
> *I shall feel that I have*
> *worked with God.*

Or think of a Swahili saying: "To those who are gracious to fellow humans, God is gracious also." Mother Teresa tells us that true love is about selfless giving. She says, "Prayer in action is love, and love in action is service. Try to give unconditionally whatever a person needs in the moment. The point is to do *something*, however small, and show you care through your actions by giving your time. We are all God's children so it is important to share His gifts."

Hazel is a woman for whom Spirituality and Outreach combine, for it is through her church that she finds a channel for her outreach needs. Hazel, at fifty-four, is no stranger to loss. When Hazel was but a child, she lost both her brother and her sister to childhood diseases. Later, while married to an abusive husband, her child died, at the age of nine, from leukemia. She eventually left that husband and ten years later remarried, having two more children. This marriage was one of great love and deep affection. After ten years, her husband died. That was eight years ago. Hazel cried as she told me, "The loss of his companionship was what was so hard. I needed his companionship and support. It was the loss of my best friend. He really was that, my best friend. I was very, very lucky to have had such a good friend for such a long time. I miss reading a book and sharing it with him, talking to him."

But Hazel is a fighter, a survivor. She tells me that her faith sustains her, her relationship with God is a source of her strength. And she gives service. For Hazel that means pouring her energies into the outreach programs in her church. She volunteers on virtually every committee. She has served as president of the Women's Association. She chairs task forces. She leads educational programs. She is a pillar of strength in the church community, always reaching out to those who suffer. She told me, "You have to continue to live life, and you have to get out of yourself, you have to be generative because that generativity heals you. You give, but you get. I enjoy working on committees. I like doing things that benefit people. If you invest in life, then you're not walking toward death. You become more than just a widow. It doesn't mean that you're not grieving over something—it doesn't mean that I haven't sustained a tremendous amount of loss, because I have. It doesn't mean that I'm not lonely either. But it means that I'm working to be out in life and to be alive."

Legacy to Your Loved One

But while Outreach may in many ways be implicitly or explicitly spiritual, the two pathways don't have to be connected. I met several people who would not describe themselves as particularly religious or spiritual, and yet they absolutely make their losses meaningful through the pathway of Outreach. Consider Hope. Her Outreach example has left a living legacy to her mother.

Hope Edelman hit a nerve with her widely acclaimed and well-received book, *Motherless Daughters*. As a motherless daughter herself, she let motherless daughters everywhere know that losing your mother is not something that you ever "get over." It affects you forever and resurfaces during key developmental periods in your life. Hope validated what I describe as Synthesis, that the love and the loss are with you always.

Religion and spirituality are not central to how Hope has made and continues to make meaning out of her mother's death. Instead, her book inspired a nationwide movement of Outreach. After her book was published, Hope began to receive hundreds, and later thousands, of letters from motherless daughters all across the world.

Then I started getting letters from women who had read the book, most of whom just wanted to thank me and tell me their stories as well. The effect the book seemed to have on women was that, after reading the stories of other women and after reading my own story, they felt compelled to share their own. A lot of those letters asked me if I knew of any support groups that I could recommend to them.

About the same time that the first book came out [a subsequent book was published in 1995—a compilation of some of these letters, called *Letters from Motherless Daughters*], Gail Eisenberg, who was interviewed in my first book, asked me out to coffee and told me about her idea of starting an organization to service this need, to initially start support groups in New York City. I was dead set against it from the start. I did not want to take on that amount of work or that amount of responsibility. But the more I thought about it—and I gave myself a few weeks to really think about it—the more I realized it was a continuing legacy to my mother, to be able to do this, to reach out and help more people. That's part of the reason why I agreed to help form the organization.

They organized a team of six women, two who were mental health professionals, and created a model for the Motherless Daughters support groups. They ran the first two groups in New York City in the fall of 1994. These were so successful that they did a few more. Then they contracted with mental health professionals in various cities throughout the United States to run these groups according to the Motherless Daughters model. They incorporated as an organization to standardize the work being done. At last count, approximately seven hundred members receive the Motherless Daughters newsletter, and support groups are held in eighteen cities nationwide. Hope's book essentially spawned a national movement.

Letters still come in and now they go to the organization. This organization is done out of pure altruism. That's the most exciting part, I think, to realize that there are women out there who will help other women in this enormously important way without any financial compensation. To go in the office and see the map of the U.S. with all the red pushpins in the cities where we have support groups either operating or about to begin is the payback. For those of us who are doing it, that's enough.

Hope described that doing the volunteer work is enormously satisfying, but that it has an additional benefit—it keeps her connected to her mother.

My mother herself was a very charitable person. She volunteered for every committee, every organization, never got paid a penny for any of her work, and I always admired that about her. Even at our worst moments, even when I was angry at her for spending four week nights a week at various volunteer meetings, I always admired that she had the capacity to be that selfless. And I wanted to be able to adopt some of that myself. In high school, I did key club, which was a volunteer organization, and in college, I volunteered for a hospice, and the same thing later in Iowa City at a free medical clinic—I've always tried to make volunteer work part of my life. Now it's a half-time job, which is fine, because I understand its importance and I do feel very much that I remain connected to my mother by doing volunteer and charitable work, by supporting organizations that I believe in, because she embodied that in her own life.

Doing this work keeps me connected to my mother. It's the satisfaction of knowing that I'm doing some good, the very visceral awareness that I am being of service to others in a positive way, which is how my mother raised me to be.

When I asked Hope if she believed that something positive had occurred out of her mother's death, she hesitantly said, "Sure, sure." I asked if her hesitancy meant it was hard to say that.

No, it's not hard to say, but I always feel that I need to qualify that because the truth is that I feel incredibly honored to have written this book. I wish it had been written thirteen years earlier so I could have benefited from it at the time of my mother's loss or shortly thereafter. I'm thrilled by the organization that's formed as a result. I'm ecstatic that we're able to help so many women. I wish we could help more, and one day if we get more resources perhaps we will be able to. Would I trade it all in a minute to have my mother back? Of course. [Here Hope gets teary-eyed. I ask if the tears surprise her.] No, the tears are fine, but realizing that I'd give it all up, that I'd give up my whole life, really, the life that I've created for myself, to have her back.

Hope reminds us that all the gains of Transcendence would be traded in a second, if only to have our loved ones back. But given that we can't, what good can come of the loss? Transcendence. Making meaning through Outreach not only benefits you the griever, but also the recipients, and ultimately our society as a whole.

Time and Outreach

Outreach evolves as time passes. Hope's ability to help and relate has changed over time. She suggests that time has been a critical variable in her ability to truly reach out to others.

> I cry sometimes in the support groups when I hear other women's stories, because I understand their pain and I feel for them. That's a significant difference that's occurred in my life over the past few years, the ability to empathize with other people's pain without immediately relating it to my own. I have led Motherless Daughters support groups in the past, I'm finishing one now, and several of the women in the group have lost mothers to cancer [as did Hope]. One woman was relating the last few weeks of her mother's life and it was very emotional, she was crying, several members of the group were crying with her, and I was crying too because it was just so sad and so moving. And I realized that I was crying because of the pain that *she* had suffered, and I understood the pain she had suffered because I'd had similar experiences when my mother was so ill. But I wasn't crying for me; I was crying for her.
>
> I'm thankful for the opportunity to have been able to achieve that, because six or seven years ago, I was very much only capable of crying for myself. It really is an issue of neediness, isn't it? I think I was very

needy six or seven years ago. I needed to focus on myself in order to validate my own loss, and I got that
through writing my book, and now it's time to go out
and help other people get to a similar point or a point
beyond one which I may have achieved, depending on
the individual.

In the initial stages of grief, you're not capable of giving,
you need to draw in and focus on the self. That's why Outreach shouldn't be attempted too early. Eliza tried to give
before she was emotionally able, and it just didn't work. She
is a thirty-three-year-old woman who lost her first child in
utero, ten years ago. She was in for her routine eighth month
pregnancy checkup, when the doctors and nurses couldn't
find a heartbeat. The baby was dead.

After the initial shock, depression set in. Eliza was incapable of doing much of anything except feeling her pain.
And yet, Eliza's rabbi called her just eight weeks after her
tragedy to see if she could speak to another young woman
who had just experienced the same thing. Eliza recalls,

I was really hurting, but I was trying to get on with
my life and putting on a good face. Then my rabbi
asked me if I would visit her. I remember looking forward to meeting somebody who I could get out of myself for, to get away from my self-pity so I could be
helpful to her. I thought that might be helpful for me.
So we met. She was so thin and pale and in denial. She
acted like it hadn't happened. So we started to get to
know each other first and then gradually I began to
bring it up. But I couldn't even hear her. We had both
just been through the same thing and yet we were each

so caught up in our own grief that we really couldn't help each other. I would tell her everything was okay and then I would break down and realize that it's not okay. Sometimes we just cried together.

Eliza wasn't ready for Outreach because she was still in the throes of Disorganization herself. You must go through the stages of healing, letting grief run its course before you move on to Transcendence.

Although I'm saying time is a critical issue in traveling along this pathway, I think it's worth mentioning that there are a few exceptions. One of the most profound and dramatic exceptions, a form of Outreach that must be acted on quite promptly, is the act of organ donation. This is a concrete way for a griever to give to others, to literally give the gift of life.

In 1993, on an average weekday afternoon, commuters were making their routine ways home to Long Island after a workday in New York City. On the Long Island Rail Road, some commuters read, some dozed, others mentally reviewed their days or planned their dinners. That is, until the quiet was shattered by a madman and a spate of stray bullets. Five people were killed that afternoon, among them twenty-seven-year-old Amy Federici.

In the midst of their pain, Amy's parents decided to donate her organs. Amy's heart and two kidneys have given life to three people who otherwise might have died. Amy's life, her death, has extended life to others. Amy's parents, the Lociceros, have become close friends with the organ recipients and have found some solace in the fact that their daughter's death had meaning. Incidentally, the Lociceros have become staunch advocates for two causes (the pathway of Reinvestment): organ donation and gun control. And they have also followed in the path of Spirituality in that they are born-again Christians. Rather than becoming bitter, they have used their faith to be forgiving. They forgive the man who murdered their daughter and even pray for his soul. This family has taken the SOAR route for healing.

Other organ donors echo the Lociceros' words. They talk about wanting something good to come out of something tragic. Tina, whose three-and-a-half-year-old daughter died in 1990, donated her child's organs after her daughter was declared brain dead. Tina said, "Just knowing that through your child's death you're giving hope and dreams to someone else helps tremendously." This is a profound and selfless gift of life, a powerful example of Outreach, and it does give solace to the families because it makes an otherwise senseless death have some meaning.

Meaning through Outreach

Whether you're helping one person or a hundred people, giving is healing, meaningful, and transcendent. In the beautiful words of Emily Dickinson,

> If I can stop one heart from breaking
> I shall not live in vain.
> If I can ease one life the aching
>   or cool one pain,
>   or help one fainting robin
>   unto his nest again,
> I shall not live in vain.

And Outreach is dynamic; it changes over time. Perhaps one year you start a grief group in your community to help others. Another year you volunteer at a hospital. Later you decide to offer your business talents in pro bono work. The options are limitless. Or maybe it's just in your daily interaction with the world—you help someone who dropped his grocery bags, you return someone's lost wallet. You allow a more compassionate nature to radiate from you, touching all in your path.

Because of your loved one's death, you are in a unique position to reach out and make a difference in this world. This is what gives meaning to death. This is what gives meaning to life. And in the words of Loretta Girzarlis, an American writer and educator, "If someone listens, or stretches out a hand, or whispers a kind word of encouragement, or attempts to understand a lonely person, extraordinary things begin to happen."

CHAPTER 8

Attitude: Healthy Thinking

---

*The road uphill and the road downhill
are one and the same.*
—HERACLITUS

When I was younger and had just moved to New York City, I met a young man who told me that he had discovered the absolute key to happiness, the key to a successful life. "What is it?" I asked, eagerly awaiting enlightenment. He said simply, "PMA." I inquired further, "What is PMA?" still eager to know his secret. He replied, "Positive Mental Attitude." "Oh that," I thought, disappointed.

Oh that little thing. It just so happens that Positive Mental Attitude has been credited for many things—from reducing stress to improving relationships, from increasing self-esteem to curing cancer. Norman Vincent Peale writes persuasively about " the power of positive thinking" in his book by the same name. Bernie Segal has attested to the miraculous ways that one's thought patterns can actually influence one's health, including creating and curing terminal illnesses. The power of one's thoughts is seemingly limitless.

Perhaps you're thinking PMA is overly touted as the cure-all of the century and that the power of one's attitude only goes so far, and perhaps you're right. But I can tell you, that just as it has a positive influence on your self-esteem, your health, and your happiness level, attitude has an unmistakable and powerful influence on your long-term grieving capacity.

I think most of us intuitively understand what is implied by attitude—the outlook we have on an issue, the stand that we take toward something, the energy that we project about an incident or idea. Webster's dictionary defines attitude as "a manner assumed indicative of one's feeling or opinion." So it's the feeling or opinion—the *belief*—below the surface that actually dictates the attitude. Attitude is a natural outgrowth of one's belief system.

Your belief system lays the foundation and determines your attitude toward life. The beliefs that you have about life, about how the world works, about God, about love, about death, these beliefs all affect your attitude toward loss.

Transcendent Attitude

When I was in college, I remember having a rather intense and mildly heated discussion with a friend about the cliché "Every cloud has a silver lining." She kept coming up with terrible life circumstances where there just couldn't possibly be a silver lining. I kept maintaining that the lining might be subtle, but that it was possible to exist in every situation. I guess even then I was beginning to formulate my ideas on Transcendence. But let's say you, like my friend, still categorically deny that this is possible. Let's say you just can't and won't buy it. I urge you to read on and to suspend your disbelief. Listen to how others have used their attitudes to reach Transcendence. Allow yourself to remain open to possibility.

Let's first look at Barbara, our SOAR traveler. So far we have seen how Barbara uses Spirituality and Outreach to make meaning out of the death of her thirty-one-year-old brother. She has gotten closer to God and developed a richer faith in her life (Spirituality). She has started support groups for bereaved siblings, she volunteers in the gay community, and she promotes giving as healing (Outreach). Now let's look at how her transcendent attitude gives meaning to her loss. She says, "I do feel that out of Bobby's death, which was horrible, there were many gifts that have grown that wouldn't have happened otherwise." What a powerful statement! In other words, her attitude reflects that good can come from bad, that meaning can be made from tragedy, that lemonade can be made from lemons. She looks for the gifts because she believes they are possible. She continues,

> Yes, [after the death of a loved one] your life is changed forever. It becomes part of the texture of who you are; in that sense you never get over it . . . but that's not necessarily a bad thing. You definitely heal, but your grief and your loss become part of the very rich texture of who you are as a human being. You can't take that away, it's just there, but it's not a bad thing that it be there. In my experience, it's been a positive thing and certainly for the Sisters [in her support groups] it's been a positive thing. . . .
>
> I have received so many gifts, really. First of all the knowledge that we are all connected, second of all that

we are in some way guided to heal, that the force is for healing and that if we allow ourselves, that is there and whether we want to call it God or energy or whatever, it doesn't really matter. Also, the people that have come into my life, the gay community that I became involved with, beautiful people. My heart was broken open, broken wide open and now I'm available to life and to people in a way that I never was before. My heart truly, truly goes out to others.

Barbara's transcendent attitude, her belief that gifts and growth are possible, frees her up to experience the lessons learned as a result of her brother's death.

It may seem incredible, overwhelming even, to hear about this transcendent attitude. All I can say is that if you let it, over time, it can develop. If you allow yourself to grieve fully and deeply in the stages of Disorganization and Reconstruction, then healing will make a transcendent attitude possible. Barbara says,

In the groups, I have to be very careful about discussing the gifts of grief. Lots of them [grievers] are really angry and if I said it, it would either make no sense or just really piss them off. If somebody in the group brings it up, that something amazing happened— and it does far more often than it doesn't—when the subject is opened, then I say, "It may be very hard for the rest of you to believe, but this is not unusual."

Every time I gave a reading, somebody would come up to me and tell me their story of some wonderful gift, some wonderful encounter, each of them the same way, looking around to make sure no one was listening, and then whispering, "You know, I had an amazing experience." But I'm very careful, because you have to wait until people are ready to share an experience, otherwise I would just come across as another of the grief bosses. I don't want to tell them great gifts grow from this if they aren't ready to hear it. But I see them experiencing it, I see it happen. If you're open, it does happen.

Barbara's positive attitude has enabled her to recognize the gifts that her loss has brought. But some people can never accept that good can come from their loss. Does this mean they can never reach Transcendence? Not necessarily. There are many other attitudes in life, attitudes that may not be explicitly "positive" and yet they ultimately lead to growth and meaning. The rest of this chapter will introduce you to attitudes that are implicitly transcendent in that they reflect new growth.

Attitude of Neutrality

In his poem "If," Rudyard Kipling describes the various beliefs and postures one must have to become "a man." One of them is:

> If you can meet with Triumph and Disaster
>   and treat those two impostors just the same, . . .
> Then yours is the Earth and everything that's in it.

Kipling implies that you should be dispassionately neutral toward both triumph and disaster, that this is the mature attitude. Rachel believes this also. I introduced you to Rachel in chapter 6, discussing her spiritual pilgrimage from Judaism to Christianity to Buddhism. She prefers to adopt an attitude that isn't especially positive or negative. And yet, in doing so, the result is ultimately transcendent. She says,

My feeling in a way is that we put much too much emphasis on good and bad experiences. Experience is experience. We are on this planet to have experiences. The fact that an experience is painful or joyous is almost irrelevant in a sense. The biggest mistake that people make is that they try to have only "good" experiences and they are crushed when they have "bad" experiences, like the death of a loved one. I'm moving much more into a realm where I'm seeing things in a much more neutral vain, that these are just phenomena of life, and you learn from them. Yes, you have feelings about them, but the feelings about them are not the most important thing. It's what meaning you ascribe to them and what you do with them subsequently.

I really think that liberating yourself from this dichotomy of feeling good and feeling bad, and painful versus pleasurable experiences, is a very important step. To not cling to things that are seen as feeling good, and to not push away things that are seen as being painful or bad, is very hard, and it takes practice. Of course our culture is totally conditioning us at every moment to seek pleasure and avoid pain. But the pain becomes less painful when you don't try to push it away, when you don't try to avoid things that we call painful. That's the only way that I've been able to deal with so much loss in my life.

I think that the greatest latitude that we have is in

taking these circumstances and having what in Buddhism is called the "right attitude" toward something. I'm not saying that I'm beyond experiencing loss and grief; I still have to feel it, but it is relativized. I say now, "What is this challenging me to do? What concepts and beliefs do I have to give up?" Having the experience of loss can be very opening and can cause a real paradigm shift within an individual.

Rachel explains to us that if you begin by looking at loss more neutrally and asking yourself, "What can I learn from this?" the result is often a transcendent conversion. You end up by learning the lessons and seeing them as gifts.

Attitude of Acceptance

Before you can see the loss neutrally, however, you first must *accept* the loss. The word acceptance is often wildly misunderstood. When I refer to acceptance, I'm not talking about acceptance in the sense of liking or approving of what happened. I'm talking about acceptance in the sense of "leaning into" what happened rather than resisting it. Pain management follows the same principles: If you resist the pain, it intensifies. If you breathe into the pain, slowly pressing into it, the pain diminishes. The flow of grief is similar over time . . . by riding the wave, allowing it to be, surrendering to the motion . . . this is the stance of receiving the grief. Once truly received, then you can choose to be positive or at least neutral toward it.

But how do you allow yourself to surrender to grief? How do you accept your loss? Rachel shares her insights on this topic:

First of all, one has to open oneself to the full experience of what the loss is. There is no way of understanding any of this stuff if we're afraid to come close to it and to confront it. I think that is the "how": by allowing contact with your own experience with your losses. The other side of loss, though, is unburdening.

All loss has the potential to be liberating on the other side. There is real truth in that. If you have the idea that the status quo, or keeping things the same all the time, is not necessarily the ideal, once you reach that level of understanding, that keeping things the same is contrary to the laws of nature and of reality, once you accept that all things are in constant flux, then the big one—death and dying—just becomes another aspect of that whole understanding.

We also learn about the attitude of acceptance from one of the most popular and admired first ladies in our history. Eleanor Roosevelt encountered multiple losses early on in her life. When she was eight, her mother died of diphtheria. Several months later, her brother Elliott died. Just two years after that, when Eleanor was ten, her beloved father died. Eleanor was devastated by these early losses and was shaped by their influence. When Eleanor was thirty-four, her grandmother (who was her primary caretaker after her parents' deaths) died. She was also deeply affected by this loss.

And yet her attitude of acceptance was extremely powerful. She said, "I believe that all we go through must have some value and therefore must have some reason. Exactly what happens, I've never been able to decide. There is a future, of that I am sure. And I have come to feel that it doesn't really matter very much because whatever the future

holds, you have to face it when you come to it, just as whatever life holds for you, you have to face in exactly the same
way. You gain strength, courage, and confidence by every
experience in which you really stop to look fear in the face.
You will be able to say to yourself, 'I lived through this
horror, I can take the next thing that comes along.' "

Attitude toward the Self

Eleanor Roosevelt, in the passage quoted above, was describing another of the transcendent attitudes, that of seeing
yourself as a survivor. The defeatist attitude is to define
yourself as a victim and a victim only. As one griever said,
"I constantly have to fight the 'poor pitiful Pearl' syn-
drome." But she does fight it. Certainly many grievers are
legitimate victims of violent crime, cruel accidents, and unusual twists of fate. But to see yourself as a victim and *only*
a victim is to live a life choked by self-pity and martyrdom.

The life-renewing transcendent attitude is to define yourself as a survivor, to see yourself as stronger, wiser, and more
compassionate. This attitude is to know that you have deeper
reservoirs of strength than you ever thought possible. Lacy
is a thirty-seven-year-old woman who suffered two miscarriages. In her words we can hear that she has survived her
losses and has come out a better person for them.

I'm willing to say now that there are some blessings
in these occurrences. As much as I desire to have a
child, it's okay if I never can. Having two miscarriages
makes you wonder if it will ever happen. But I think
that through [taking] this as an exercise, or as a lesson,
or one of life's occurrences, it molds me in a direction

that's going to help me in the long run, to help myself and help other people. You don't learn too much when you're fat and happy. Things get your attention when you're in pain. I'd much rather choose lessons that are easy, of course. But I do feel that we're guided through certain occurrences in our lives in order to build and shape and mold us into better beings. It has really humbled me in a way.

Another griever told me, "The grief broke me and then out of that I became stronger. I see myself more as a whole human being. If I survived this, I can survive anything." Belief translates to reality with this type of attitude, for if you believe that you have become stronger, wiser, and more compassionate, then indeed you have become so.

Attitude toward Life

After you lose someone precious to you, you never see life in the same way again. The bubble of security, and perhaps innocence, has been burst. You know that life is precious, brief, and oh so fragile. But what do you do with such vulnerability? One attitude is to live your life with fear and paranoia. Another response is to embrace the fleeting quality of life by seizing the day (carpe diem) and never taking things for granted.

The transcendent attitude toward life knows there is no time for procrastination, no time for putting off important goals. Life is just too short. As one bereaved mother told me, "Life is all a big classroom and everything has lessons in it. But don't forget that this life is just a blink of an eye."

When you see life as precious, fragile, brief, fleeting, the transcendent attitude is to take advantage of every moment, to make every moment matter. There simply is no time to put things off until tomorrow, for tomorrow may never come. It can cause in you a fierce desire to make every moment count. It can inspire a savoring and appreciation of life that other people don't have. Death can make you stop procrastinating. One griever said after her father died, "His death makes me want to live a full life and do the things I want to do. My father was always waiting for the big break. He always lived on expectation . . . always. He never lived in today. Today is what I want. He always had a plan in the works, and he didn't do any of them. He died before any of his plans came to fruition. I don't want to live that way; I want to live now and do the things that I want to do. I'm not going to wait to do them, because I don't know what's going to happen."

Death can also stimulate a reprioritizing of life, a reexamination of what's important and what isn't. When you have lost that which is most important to you, nothing else matters. All those things that were once so crucial—getting that promotion, buying a new car, losing ten pounds—become irrelevant.

Christina, whose grown son died five years ago said, "Four weeks after Robby left his body, our apartment was robbed. But you know, it just didn't matter. It wasn't that big a deal. We put value on these material things and they just don't matter."

Another griever echoed, "After a major loss, you see what's really important in life for the first time; you realize life is not about money or having more education than your neighbors. It's about love between people. And every moment of life is like a precious jewel. Once you see that, you can never go back." Another griever said, "There are so few things that are important in life. Relationships are important and really being happy. Making a lot of money, having a big house—it doesn't matter. The way you are inside and how much you love yourself and if you're able to do whatever it is that you want to do. That's what matters." Loss can inspire a richer savoring and appreciation of what is meaningful in life.

Attitude toward Death

For most of us death is the grim reaper, the black shadow, the ultimate enemy to be fought at all costs. But for many grievers, after the death of a loved one, death is no longer such a demon. Death is seen as a peaceful doorway, a spiritual transition tunnel that stirs images of freedom and awe rather than fear and terror. Some see death as a relief or, as one widow I know calls death now, "an old friend."

Christina continued discussing her son's death and said, "I had to read *Emmanuel* [*Emmanuel's Book*, by Pat Rodegast and Judith Stanton], very sweet and very gentle. It said, 'Death is like taking off a tight shoe, it's such a relief' and 'Death is like being in a stuffy room and you walk out into a beautiful green, refreshing environment.' I had to hear that. It helped and was so comforting. Now, I miss Robby's body, but the essence of Robby will always be with me. The resurrection means there is no death. The form may change but the content is the same."

Others say, "I have no fear of death now because I know she is waiting for me." Some say they look forward to death, welcome it since it will provide a heavenly reunion. Harry Scott Holland, canon of St. Paul's Cathedral around the turn

of the century, wrote the following poem, "What Is Death?"
A griever brought it to one of my bereavement groups to
share with her fellow sojourners.

Death is nothing at all. I have only slipped away into
the next room. I am I and you are you. Whatever we
were to each other, that we are still. Call me by my old
familiar name. Speak to me in the easy way which you
always used. Put no difference in your tone. Wear no
forced air of solemnity or sorrow. Laugh as we always
laughed at the little jokes we enjoyed together. Play,
smile, think of me, pray for me. Let my name be ever
the household word that it always was. Let it be spoken
without effect, without the trace of a shadow on it. Life
means all that it ever meant. It is the same that it ever
was. There is absolutely unbroken continuity. Why
should I be out of mind because I am out of sight?

I am waiting for you, for an interval, somewhere very
near, just around the corner. All is well.

I briefly mentioned Beverly in chapter 5, whose thirty-
three-year-old daughter died of AIDS. She told me that she
will never think of death in the same way because now she
knows there's another spiritual life after this one.

I was with Iris in the hospital and she was dying. I
whispered to her, "Please show me that there's more."
It was on Saturday morning, and the doctor said, "It's
going to be any minute." I was at her bed, and there
was a nurse and two other mothers with me. And all
of a sudden, every part of her body moved, her legs
one at a time came up, and I mean high, the hand came

up very high, each arm, her shoulders, her head came off the bed, and then her mouth opened up and she died. I said to the nurse, "What's happening?" The nurse didn't know. One of the mothers said, "I think we're watching her spirit leaving her body." And that's exactly what it was. She showed me that there was something more. If anybody in this world could have done it, she could have. She showed me because she knew I needed it.

Other grievers have told me that they felt or saw their loved one's spirits depart. Most everyone described this as a comforting phenomenon. Believing that there's something on the other side of death makes your attitude more calm and less fearful. As one griever who lost her son said, "I used to think death was the worst thing that could happen to me. Now I'm not afraid of dying. If he can do it, I can do it. And I might even see him again."

Attitude of Perspective

Perspective means you take that proverbial step backward to view your life from a distance, to see how every event is a piece of the puzzle, how each of us are but cogs in the wheel of life. As one young widow said, "I came to realize that we all come and we all go . . . flowers live and they die. Everything has a life cycle."

An older widow, Sally, lost her husband and both parents. She said, "I walked the beach after my mother died. I walked the beach through the grief. I wanted to be a sea gull. Water is amazing. I saw those waves and I thought to myself, millions of people have walked by these waves and they're all dead. And I'm going to be dead too and the waves just keep coming in and out. That was healing to me."

There's something healing about transcending the self, about lifting out of the muck and rising to the radiant clouds above. From there, everything looks different. Everything seems less weighty. Perspective provides solace.

Margaret is a seventy-year-old-woman who lived through the most unthinkable of tragedies: she lost not one but two sons, ages three and five, within nine months of each other. Her attitude of perspective helped her cope. She said, "I went to Greece for a year in 1956 when my third son was three years old. In those days, Greece was very poor. It helped me because, for one, their life was not so modern. The rhythm of life was very different and you realized that they've lived there for two thousand years, three thousand years. People die and people are born and it goes on and on and on, world without end. So that sort of helped me."

An attitude of perspective lifts you out of yourself and out of your present circumstances. It means that you deflect a narcissistic, self-involved focus to gain a larger vision of life and your place in it. This attitude is a critical one in leading to Transcendence since it so clearly embodies the potential of what can occur over time—a shift from focusing inward to focusing outward.

Attitude of Gratitude

It may be hard to imagine feeling grateful after the death of someone near and dear to your heart. But it's possible to feel grateful for the love that you did share, however briefly.

Kim is a remarkable woman who lost her only daughter to an unusual brain seizure more than fifteen years ago. After the death of her daughter, Kim decided to go back to school to study psychology. For her dissertation, she researched the issue of losing an only child as a distinct type of bereavement that includes the additional loss of one's role as parent. She interviewed bereaved parents, one of whom said, "When I remember that Lynne was a gift, pure and simple, something I neither earned or deserved nor had a right to. And when I remember that the appropriate response to a gift, even when it is taken away, is gratitude, then I am better able to try and thank God that I was ever given her in the first place."

And Kim herself wrote in the preface to her doctoral dissertation, "My daughter died on July 9, 1982, three weeks before her ninth birthday. Losing Lynne has changed my life in many ways. I cherish my memories of our time together, and I value highly the impact she has had on my life, both in her coming and in her going."

One way to feel gratitude, then, is to be grateful for what you had. Another way to secure the attitude of gratitude is to appreciate what you have left. One griever whose daughter died in the tragic Oklahoma City bombing of 1995 clipped from the newspaper a prayer that she recites daily. The prayer goes, "Help us, Lord, when we are faced with a loss, to be grateful for what we have." She said this reminds her to focus on her surviving children, to focus on the living.

Another griever who lost her son in a multiple shooting at a McDonald's in 1984 said that she still struggles with the sadness of the loss of her beloved child. But a very beautiful and poignant adage helps her to maintain an attitude of gratitude. She advises, "There's a saying: Yesterday is history, tomorrow's a mystery, and today is a gift, which is why it's called the present. I like that a lot." She adds that you shouldn't waste a gift when it's as precious as the present.

I think it's also worth mentioning that countless of the grievers who shared their experiences with me mentioned their gratitude for the love and support of friends and family members and even for the kindness of strangers. Many, many people told me that they wouldn't have survived but for the support of friends, ministers, rabbis, surviving family members, and new-found support networks of other grievers. Again, we are not alone; we are all connected. An attitude of gratitude for this supportive connection focuses one's energy in a positive rather than a negative way.

Attitude toward Suffering

They say that death and taxes are the only certainties in life. But pain and suffering are an integral part of life as well. So when a loss occurs, the real question is not "Why did this happen?" but "Why did you think it wouldn't?"

But the key to one's attitude toward suffering is more than just accepting its inevitability, it lies in how one manages the suffering and whether one can make it meaningful. Victor Frankl, in his book *Man's Search for Meaning*, writes that one of the ways a human being can find meaning in his life is by the stand that he takes toward suffering. He says, "Through the right attitude, unchangeable suffering is transmuted into a heroic and victorious achievement. . . . Even the helpless victim of a hopeless situation, facing a fate he cannot change, may rise above himself, may grow beyond himself, and by so doing change himself. He may turn a personal tragedy into a triumph." Frankl goes on to give an example of this phenomenon.

Once, an elderly general practitioner consulted me because of his severe depression. He could not overcome the loss of his wife who had died two years before and whom he had loved above all else. . . . I confronted him with the question, "What would have happened, Doctor, if you had died first, and your wife would have had to survive you?" "Oh," he said, "For her this would have been terrible; how she would have suffered!" Whereupon I replied, "You see, Doctor, such suffering has been spared her, and it was you who have spared her this suffering—to be sure, at the price that now you have to survive and mourn her." He said no word but shook my hand and calmly left my office. In some way, suffering ceases to be suffering at the moment it finds a meaning, such as the meaning of a sacrifice.

Of course, this was no therapy in the proper sense since, first, his despair was no disease; and second, I could not change his fate; I could not revive his wife. But in that moment I did succeed in changing his *attitude* toward his unalterable fate inasmuch as from that time on he could at least see a meaning in his suffering.

I think this is a lovely example of finding meaning in suffering. And Frankl points out a critical feature: it is the attitude that we *choose* to take, the attitude that we decide to adopt that will make the fate meaningful. We are self-determining in that respect. In other words, you cannot change the reality of what happened, but you can definitely change how you ultimately respond to it. As Frankl says, "Everything can be taken away from a human being except the last freedom, the freedom to choose your attitude in response to the circumstances in your life."

The attitudes toward grief can be learned. They require conscious choice and determined, willful harnessing. For some, a positive attitude comes easily, effortlessly. For these lucky souls, a positive attitude seems naturally bred into their pleasant dispositions. But for most of us, a positive attitude must be cultivated. It must be nurtured and nourished much as a gardener tends his tender plants. For many of us, a positive attitude needs to be carefully coaxed and deliberately cajoled into being. But attitude *can be learned* if it doesn't happen naturally. It is a conscious choice, enforced by desire and will.

It takes hard work to cultivate a transcendent attitude. Through reading, thinking, talking, reflecting, therapy, grief work, and so on—with the help of all these tools, you can consciously work to shape your attitude. But remember that underneath it all, at the core of these transcendent concepts, lies the fundamental belief that life is worth living. Coming to believe in life, in love, and in the future is what eventually takes the griever to a pinnacle pathway of Transcendence, the pathway of Reinvestment.

The Woven SOAR Tapestry

Before we continue, let's stop to take stock. I've been telling you about the pathways that lead to Transcendence and make meaning out of life and out of death. Some grievers choose one pathway, others choose several. While it is not necessary to follow each of the four pathways, one's journey is fortified if more than one pathway is traveled. While one strand of thread is strong, bound with another strand it becomes stronger still. Multiple strands create rich fabrics of strength and endurance. I want to share with you an example of Mary, a woman who suffered two tragic losses in her life, the death of her teenage daughter and the death of her husband after twenty-five years of marriage. Let's analyze how she embodies each of the pathways we have discussed thus far.

It was the summer of 1983. Mary was vacationing on the beach with her husband, Tim, her two teenage daughters, and her daughters' friend. Darcy was a senior in high school with exciting plans to attend her state's university in the fall. Lisa had just finished her first year of high school. One day the girls decided to go into town to shop while Mary stayed behind to catch up on her reading. At about 5:00 P.M., Mary heard loud sirens. She remembers hearing the ambulance and wondering what had happened. Little did she know that the car carrying her two daughters and their friend had just been hit broadside by a truck going 65 MPH.

After a while, when the girls didn't come home, Mary started to get worried and wondered why they were late. So she called the police telling them that they were vacationing in the area, three teenage girls were missing, and that maybe they had gotten lost. The police asked for the car's license number and hung up. They called back in minutes telling her that the car had been in an accident, the girls were in the hospital, it was very serious, and that she should come right away. Mary told me,

> I called Tim, who hadn't joined us yet but he already had heard what had happened. Lisa had been conscious at the scene of the accident and had given the police Tim's number at home. Tim told me that the police said that one of the girls had died but they didn't know

which one it was. I told him I'm on my way to the hospital. He told me to call as soon as I knew. I didn't have a car so they sent a police car to get me. It's so weird how composed you can be when something like this happens.

They first took me to a family room. I said, "I already know that one of the girls died, which one was it?" It was the girls' friend. She was on the passenger side and was killed instantly. Meanwhile Darcy and Lisa were in critical condition and had sustained massive injuries.

First they took me in to see Darcy. She was in a coma and that just wiped me out. Then they took me up to see Lisa. Lisa's jaw was broken in two places, her pelvis was broken in two places, all of her ribs were cracked, her lungs had collapsed, and her liver was torn. Lisa was on her way into surgery. I had to sign release forms. After I saw Lisa, I just collapsed. I thought I was going to throw up. It was so overwhelming. I collapsed on the floor in the bathroom, and all I remember is this lady doctor who just held me on the floor for I have no idea how long.

For the next two months both girls were in critical condition; it was one roller coaster ride after another. Darcy was in a coma from the very beginning and nearly died on several occasions. I remember in May writing to her university where she was supposed to be a freshman that fall and saying that she wouldn't be able to come this year. It never occurred to me that she would never go. I thought they would both pull through. I couldn't accept that they would die. It all happened so fast. It's amazing how just one second can change so many lives. So many lives just changed forever in a split second.

Lisa eventually recovered from her physical injuries, but Darcy stayed in the coma. When I met with Mary in 1992, it was exactly nine years after the accident and Darcy was still in the coma. Darcy had been in hospitals for several years, had lived at home with nursing care for many years, and had just recently been moved to a special care facility.

After the accident, Mary told me that she and Tim were brought closer together. They had always had a close marriage, but she said, "it put some meaning in our lives, a focus that we had to pull together to work through this." Tim founded the local chapter of the National Head Injury Association. She told me, "He was really into 'if you're going to have to be in this kind of situation, let's do what you can to make it better for other people.' At that time, I was more into 'let's do everything we can for Darcy.' He probably accepted what the situation was sooner than I did and knew that there wasn't much hope for Darcy. He wanted to channel his energy into a positive cause." Later he was elected to the board of directors of the National Head Injury Association.

But just three years after the accident, Tim was diagnosed with lung cancer. Two years after that, he died. It came as a shock. Mary said, "We didn't expect it to be that fast. I knew there was no cure, but I thought we could handle it with medicine and remission. I thought it would shorten his life, but I had no idea that it would be that short. For forty-seven years, nothing bad had ever happened to me. . . . To lead a very ordinary life and then all of a sudden . . . and it wasn't just Darcy and Tim, it was also my mother who died in September after the accident and Tim's father who died. I couldn't absorb it all."

How does anyone absorb it all? As Mary said, "You take it one day at a time." As the days added up, as time passed, she worked through the Shock, the Disorganization, the Reconstruction. She has come to accept Synthesis in her life. And she has even had flashes of Transcendence. First of all, she has a strong spiritual life. She said, "I have always had a very basic faith. I've never been outwardly demonstrative at all but I've always had a very solid, basic faith. And I pray more now. I think my basic prayer is, 'Lord, help me grow into the person that you created me to be,' and that's kind of scary because then you really do have to accept things, and I just hope I have the courage to do it. I think that we're all here for a reason, for some reason . . . some times we never know what that reason is, but that's okay."

Mary also followed the pathway of Outreach. After Tim died, the National Head Injury Association asked her to fulfill his term. She did and was later elected to be president. Although no longer president, she told me she expects to be involved with that organization on some level forever, in order to help others.

Mary is a remarkable, inspirational woman, but it is her attitude that impresses me as one of her strongest pathways toward Transcendence. She has a different attitude toward life, she has an attitude of gratitude, and she has an attitude of conscious choice.

I think it helps to have a grateful heart. There's always something to be thankful for. Even in the worst of circumstances, there's always something. . . . And a sense of humor. Right after the accident, we'd be in the midst of this terrible thing, and we would just break out laughing. That's life. There's pathos and there's joy all the time.

I have even more of a grateful heart now. I appreciate people and life in general. It never occurred to me before, the fragility of life. You just take things for granted until you've gone through something like this. I don't take things for granted anymore. Oh, and I am so grateful for the support and love I receive from friends and family.

I've known people who became bitter after a tragedy, and I didn't want to be like that. I made a conscious effort not to be. Getting involved has helped. I've met a lot of people who get isolated from their communities; they have a completely different outlook. So I try to stay involved. I really had a specific feeling of not wanting to be isolated and a conscious feeling of not wanting to be bitter. I did things. I didn't try to do things to be happy, but you do what you're supposed to do and happiness is a result of it.

In 1993, ten years after the accident and five years after Tim's death, Darcy finally died. I spoke to Mary again, who told me that while she had many feelings about this, overall she felt relief for Darcy, who had "suffered long enough" and had "served whatever purpose that she was put here to serve." And in a succinct summary of the effects of Synthesis, Mary told me, "They [Darcy, Tim, the other loved ones who have died] will always be a part of my life. Most of the time, it's not a sad recollection. Many times I feel joy and happiness for that."

Incidentally, Mary provides a timely segue into our next

chapter on Reinvestment, since she also embodies that pathway to Transcendence by electing to reinvest in love. Mary met and married Karl in 1991. Karl lost his wife the year before Tim died, and Karl is also a bereaved parent. Mary said, "We had each gone to the same church for twenty years but we didn't know each other. A mutual friend kept encouraging us to meet. One day he called and asked me out to dinner, which totally surprised me. I thought I was young enough to remarry but I couldn't imagine the dating process."

Mary told me, "Karl and I are very happy, very compatible, but it's different. I wasn't looking for someone just like Tim. It's just different." Mary and Karl accept that their relationship is unique and different from the ones before it. And they don't try to diminish the importance of the past. They are open about their thoughts and feelings. They acknowledge the past and together build a new future. This remarkable willingness to again be vulnerable to loss, to again embrace the joys and dangers of love is true testimony to the human heart's resilience.

And it is but one of the ways to travel the final pathway toward Transcendence, the pathway of Reinvestment.

CHAPTER 9

Reinvestment: Embracing Life

———

Loss makes artists of us all as we weave new patterns in the fabric of our lives.
—GRETA W. CROSBY

Many of you may recall from your childhood a famous spider named Charlotte and a famous pig named Wilbur. I'm referring, of course, to the cherished children's story by E. B. White, called *Charlotte's Web*. It was always one of my favorite stories as a child and perhaps even foreshadowed my interest in the bereavement field. Why? Because it's not just a story about a pig at the state fair, or even about a friendship between animals. It is, in essence, a story about loss and reinvestment.

After the state fair was over and Wilbur won first prize, Charlotte (his best friend) informed him that she wouldn't be returning with him to the farm. When he inquired why not, she told him that she was going to die within a matter of days. Upon hearing this, Wilbur was crushed, grief-stricken, and torn by pain and sorrow. But in the midst of his panic, he thought of Charlotte's egg sac and the 514 little spiders due to hatch that spring. He resolved that "if Charlotte herself was unable to go home to the barn, at least he must take her children along."

So Wilbur got the egg sac and took it back with him to the barn for safekeeping. Later, Charlotte died . . . all alone; Wilbur grieved deeply. And he waited for Charlotte's eggs to hatch. Eventually, in the spring, they hatched, with hundreds of baby spiders coming out of the sac, waving to Wilbur, and then suddenly flying off with spun-silk balloons, searching for homes of their own. Wilbur was crushed when they left, until he realized that three of the baby spiders had decided to stay and weave their webs in the barn, making their home with Wilbur.

> "Welcome to the barn cellar. You have chosen a hallowed doorway from which to string your webs. I think it is only fair to tell you that I was devoted to your mother. I owe my very life to her. She was brilliant, beautiful, and loyal to the end. I shall always treasure her memory. To you, her daughters, I pledge my friendship, forever and ever."

It was a happy day for Wilbur. And many more happy, tranquil days followed.

I tell this story here because Wilbur, even while grief-stricken, chose to reinvest in the future when he decided to guard Charlotte's eggs and see that they hatched healthily. He also chose to reinvest in love when he allowed his heart to reattach to another living thing, even while knowing that a heart can and does get broken. In other words, Wilbur's response to Charlotte's death is an illustration of the fourth pathway toward Transcendence, the pathway of Reinvestment.

Reinvestment is a broad term to describe the phenomenon of connecting with life again, of caring enough to dedicate yourself to the living and to the future. But it's not just that you return to work or that you go back to your "old" life. Remember as we know from Synthesis, you are forever changed. You cannot just go back to life as if nothing has happened, because something has happened and life will never be the same. So Reinvestment really means accepting the loss and channeling your pain, creating something new that didn't exist before, creating something meaningful that is a direct result of your experience with loss.

There are many different ways of reinvesting. Some reinvest in love, others in a creative project. Some reinvest in a new career, others in a new cause or mission. You see, when your loved one was alive, you invested a certain amount of energy into your relationship with that person. When she dies, you spend a certain amount of energy grieving and mourning that person. In Transcendence, you take that same energy and you channel it into something productive, something meaningful, something full of life.

Reinvestment is, in many ways, the ultimate expression of human resilience, the consummate triumph of the human spirit. For Reinvestment means that even when loss tramples your heart and shatters your spirit, it is possible that you, like the mythical bird, the phoenix, can rise from the ashes to embrace life anew. Grievers who choose to do this are reaffirming their rightful place in a world where life, love, loss, and death coexist.

Rabbi Harold Kushner aptly put it, "We need to get over the questions that focus on the past and on the pain—'Why did this happen to me?'—and ask instead the question which opens doors to the future: 'Now that this has happened, what shall I do about it?'" This is the question that leads back to life. This is the question that leads to Reinvestment.

Reinvestment in Love

Wilbur the pig accepted his grief and then channeled his pain back out so that he could love Charlotte's children. The risk and danger, of course, both for Wilbur and for all of us, is that if we love again we may lose again. A common defense is to protect ourselves from the possibility of future losses by barricading our broken hearts. Certainly, this desire is understandable and perhaps even necessary initially. But *over time* those who keep their hearts guarded under lock and key may protect themselves from pain, but they also prevent any real joy from touching their lives. The bottom line is if you don't risk, you don't love. And without love, life can be very hollow indeed.

Loss, unfortunately, can stifle the ability to love. One example of that is a bereaved parent who loses the ability to give love to his remaining children. It's as if the parental stream of love dries up. Eva is a twenty-six-year-old woman whose brother was murdered ten years ago. She said, "After it happened, my father cut himself off from society. He freaked out, lost his job, couldn't deal with it. I haven't talked with him since 1988 and I don't even know where he is. It was like he didn't care that I was still alive—he lost both of his kids."

Although all losses are painful, and many factors contribute to make each loss personally unique and meaningful to each griever, the loss of a child is generally recognized as the most severe, the most wretched, the most awful. I hate to compare pain, but losing a child is so unexpected to parents; it's so out-of-sync with the expected life cycle, that it makes the loss especially ruinous. No parent, no matter what his age, expects to bury his own child. So perhaps it's understandable on one level that Eva's father "freaked out." But on another level, he compounded his losses by rejecting Eva. He lost both of his children.

But how do you make yourself love again when you know that the price for love is the potential for loss? Well, it's not easy. It's a process of working through the feelings; it takes time. First you have to do the grief work, because otherwise you're really not in a position to give. The example of Wilbur's reinvestment is oversimplified, but it's a child's story. The reality is that few people can or do reinvest in love so quickly without first going through the deep grieving process. Of course there are exceptions to every rule, but in general, time to grieve is required before a person should reinvest in love.

If you "love" again too quickly, it may be a way of avoiding the pain of the grief work. Widowers have a tendency to jump back into relationships before they have fully grieved because they are afraid to be alone, afraid to face the loss. But jumping into another relationship before you've grieved is not the answer. You cannot replace that which was lost. Sooner or later, one way or another, the grief must be confronted, felt, and processed.

Victoria is a widow with two children; her husband was killed in an automobile accident on New Year's Eve fifteen years ago while they were vacationing. As you can imagine, Victoria's world was shattered. Her faith, in particular, was rocked and she eventually went to seminary to search for answers. I'll be discussing her spiritual journey in more detail in chapter 10. For the purposes of analyzing reinvestment in love, I asked her what it was like to consider remarriage after such a tragic loss.

> For a while I had zero interest in remarrying. Then I thought, if I could just remarry, life will go on; I wouldn't have to go through being a single woman and being the sole supporter. I could skip over this. It was sort of a magical dream I had. But my experience was that in those first years, people began introducing me to men and it was sort of awkward. Everybody ran from me because I was so needy. Once I went through seminary and really became healed and whole—that's what spiritual union is all about, making one whole again, I became a whole person again—then suddenly I became attractive. Everyone started asking me out again. I was overwhelmed by all the invitations. What caused this? It had to be an inner wholeness and healing. I was able to love again.

Victoria alerts us to the fact that she couldn't love again until after she had completely, thoroughly done her grief work. She wasn't open to love until she had fully experienced Disorganization with all its many ramifications. It was only in allowing herself to feel the grief that she could ultimately heal.

*   *   *

Transcendent reinvestment in love does not try to replace. It recognizes the loss and accepts the changes as part of the reality of living and losing. Transcendent reinvestment in love, like Synthesis, is a process of integrating the old with the new. Victoria did eventually marry another man, with his own grown children. She told me:

In a stepfamily, as much as I'm devoted to my new husband and his children, it will never be that sense of oneness. They're not *our* children. There's no way his children will ever think of me as their mother, because I'm not. And my children will never think of him as their father, because he is not. And the house will always be a compilation, there will never be the same sense of belonging. I don't think one can replace it. One can have something different and new, but one can't ever really replace what is lost.

I'm probably willing now to integrate [my first husband's] memory and that marriage more into my life. And through my own new marriage, I can begin to hold onto the old marriage and the old ways. The pain is not completely gone. The pain of loss in fact often comes to me in very intense ways that I have to deal with still. But that experience is increasingly a source of strength after all these years. Because our commitment was fulfilled to each other, there is a strength there that I can sort of dip into now as I struggle with this new family, stepfamily, and belonging.

Victoria understands that her new marriage is not a replacement for what she lost. It is not a way to make the grief journey easier. But it is a way to embrace the future. By reinvesting in love, Victoria can transcend the loss; she can move beyond her pain and find meaning in life again.

For some, a future after the loss of a loved one seems impossible. And they can't imagine loving again. All their emotional energy is tied up in grief and anguish; they have nothing left to give anyone else. But as difficult as it is, if we can allow ourselves to reinvest, to reconnect with other people, we can begin healing and move toward Transcendence.

Consider Kim, who lost her only child, eight-year-old Lynne, to an unexpected brain seizure. Kim had a long and rocky road in grieving the loss of her daughter. She went from being suicidal (which is not an uncommon initial response in bereaved parents) and alcoholic, to being able to love again and reconnect with others. One way she does this is by teaching Sunday school to children. She tells me, "In my life I have a family now that's a church family which also includes children. It's not a replacement, certainly, for having your only child, but it's a way of appreciating and being around kids again." In other words, she's able to care and love again, and it was this reconnection that literally helped her survive.

For Kim, her tragic loss not only led her to new places in her spirituality and her capacity to love, but her loss also led her onto an entirely new career path. In fact, for many, the pathway of Reinvestment to Transcendence involves reinvesting in a new career.

Reinvestment in a New Career

I talked to countless grievers who, as a result of their tragedies, became nurses, hospice workers, bereavement counselors. On the one hand, they are acting on their desire to help others in ways that they may or may not have experienced. And on the other hand, they are benefiting from the personal healing that takes place in making one's profession a form of Outreach. Remember, Outreach is the pathway of helping others. When you want to help others to the point of making it your full-time job, then you reinvest in a career change.

Kim didn't consciously choose to become a psychologist and a bereavement professional. It evolved unexpectedly. She was a businesswoman in the corporate world and decided to pursue a doctorate in human and organizational development. Her intention was to study the five men who had left her company to start a directly competing company, and her dissertation was to be titled, "Corporate Defectors." But one day, in a hotel room while on a business trip, Kim had a revelation that changed the direction of her life.

I had what I call an epiphany experience in my hotel room. I had just bought a book called *The Process of Role Exit*, by Helen Rose Ebaugh of the University of Chicago, who had studied people—ex-prostitutes, ex-cops—and in there she had parents without custody as part of her study: what happens to these parents who have to give up custody of their kids? Instantaneously came a thought, "That's it, that's why you're still having such a difficult time; you had two losses here, you lost Lynne and you worked through the fact that she's off doing her own thing now, and you don't have to worry about her, but you've also lost the role of a mother, and that's part of who you are, and you have no way of using that in the corporate world, because

the corporate world is not terribly receptive to nurturing personalities—they're much more receptive to com-
petitive personalities."

So Kim changed her course of study from analyzing corporate defectors to analyzing the coping strategies of women
who had lost their only children. In conducting her research,
in connecting with other bereaved mothers, she found healing and meaning in her life. She also realized that she had
to leave the corporate world, a place that was forcing her to
compromise her nurturing self. So one year after she began
her doctoral program, she left her corporate job and gave
herself the gift of devoting herself full-time to completing
her dissertation on bereavement.

Kim is now a psychologist who specializes in bereavement
issues and who also writes in the field about the important
clinical distinction of a parent who loses an only child. Kim,
like myself, is interested in making meaning. Has she made
meaning out of her loss? Yes. She said,

> The fact that I can take a very difficult situation and
> try and have something good come of it by increasing
> our knowledge in the field of bereavement for the pro-
> fessional side, as well as trying to help individual par-
> ents on the other side of it stay with their anguish and
> find their own path. . . . That's meaning. That's adding
> meaning into this experience.
>
> When you are able to give up some of the pain—
> because nobody ever takes your pain away, you have
> to give it up yourself—when you give up and let loose
> of that pain, your perspective changes. You're giving
> meaning to both the life and the death. I am a totally

different person than I ever would have been if she hadn't come here. And I am also a totally different person than I ever would have been if she hadn't left when she did.

Kim found herself ultimately drawn from the corporate world into the field of mental health. For her, the process evolved unexpectedly. For others, the choice is calculated and consciously derived. Jim is an example of a transcender who, because of his tragic loss, decided to make it meaningful by consciously, systematically changing his career in order to help others.

In 1989, Jim was a sales manager for a publishing company, a job that involved a great deal of travel. He and his wife, Mary, both age thirty-nine, had just celebrated their eighteenth wedding anniversary. They had three children, who were ages eight, eleven, and fourteen at the time. Jim's father-in-law had just died and they had all attended the funeral. The next morning, the family was driving home when lightning figuratively struck. Jim told me,

About halfway through the drive, my wife went into a seizure of sorts. Her head cocked back and she started breathing in, not out but just in. I looked over and thought maybe she had a bloody nose. I asked what was wrong and then realized that something was desperately wrong. She had no history at all of any health problems; she was only thirty-nine years old. I pulled over to the side of the road, and at this point she had collapsed. Her head fell over onto me. The kids were in the backseat screaming, "What's wrong? What's wrong?" I went back on the highway and headed to the first exit and stopped at a hotel to ask where's the nearest hospital. At that point, a nurse and a doctor who were in the restaurant saw what was going on. They both came out and took her out of the car and started CPR on her, and somebody called an ambulance.

Mary died a few days later, never having regained consciousness, and Jim found that his world as he knew it was shattered. He said,

It was more than death, it was a traumatic death experience. It was all of the ramifications of that, all of the physical reactions, panic attacks, discombobulation, "where am I?" all of it. Basically at that point, and thereafter for the next few months, I looked around for some help, wanting to scream, "What the heck is this, what am I going through, and how do I help my kids?" All of a sudden I'm the one taking care of the kids. I'm a single father; I'm unmarried, and I have a job where I'm supposed to go up and down the East Coast every other day.

I went to a psychiatrist that was recommended. I went twice and I discovered that he knew very little about grief and loss. But it was a good chance to get out and talk about it, tell the story. That helped from that respect, but that's about it. After two sessions he said, "You want to come back?" I said, "I don't know, you think I should?" He said, "It's up to you." I said, "Nah, I guess not." It wasn't real helpful.

They also tried family counseling, and it was helpful to a degree, but Jim felt that the counselor really didn't have the specialization necessary to help them as fully as possible. He told me that a few months after that experience he began thinking about what it would be like to start a center specifically for offering counseling services for grief and loss issues.

But he continued his emotional struggle, and then in 1990 he met Marianne. He began dating her, overcoming the obstacles of going public with a new relationship, and slowly allowing his heart to risk loving again. Before they were married, they talked about creating a counseling center together.

> Marianne and I talked about leaving our jobs and starting this center so that people wouldn't have to go through everything I went through, or at least would be helped in the process. And so after we got married, I started going to school and then went back to school full-time and got a master's in counseling. And then she went back to school and got a master's in clinical psychology, and three years ago we opened up the center.

They created the New England Center for Loss and Transition, a nonprofit organization that offers individual and group counseling, seminars, weekend workshops, and services for bereaved children and their families. They also edit a grief newsletter for professionals in the field. And, drawing on Jim and Marianne's skills and knowledge of professional marketing, the center now runs an annual national bereavement conference that has become one of the largest of its kind. This national conference is their primary fundraiser, and it serves as a forum to educate professionals in the field so that they may be more effective mental health facilitators to other grievers.

Becoming a grief counselor to help others and running the Center for Loss and Transition has become Jim's life work and has made his loss meaningful. He said in no uncertain terms, "This center was done to create meaning for this stupid thing that happened. It was senseless and meaningless, a meaningless event in an otherwise ordered universe. So the only way that I could make meaning out of that, in my mind, was to create something like [the center]. It could have gone one of several ways; this is the way I chose. It felt like a conscious decision. It's clearly a legacy."

As much as Jim values his work, he recognizes that the center cannot and should not take over his life. He says that he and Marianne are good at monitoring each other and providing each other with the perspective necessary to balance work and play.

It's an interesting piece of the story that Jim and Marianne created the center together, they work at the center together, that it's become a bond for them in a profound and important way. When I asked Jim what was Marianne's motivation for changing her career and embarking on this adventure with him, he shared with me what she might have answered herself: "You can't be with someone this close, you can't love someone this much and not struggle with this person along the way and be at one with this person. In many ways my struggle in grief then and beyond was her struggle as well. She had wanted to someday leave corporate life and do something in human services, she just wasn't sure what, but this looked like a good entry."

Jim's reinvestment is, then, a legacy of love that looks backward toward his deceased wife and forward as well in that it's a creation of love that joins Jim with his present wife. It's a poignant example of how love, loss, and new life can intertwine.

Reinvest in a Cause

Of course not everyone has the will, desire, or opportunity to completely change their careers. Fortunately it is but one among many of the ways to reinvest. Some grievers find that they prefer to maintain their current careers but they become involved as a volunteer in a cause or a mission that speaks to their grief.

Consider the many millions of volunteers who get involved with MADD (Mothers Against Drunk Driving) or SADD (Students Against Drunk Driving) after their lives have been punctured by this type of loss. Incidentally, MADD was originally started by a mother after her thirteen-year-old daughter was killed by a drunk driver. Or consider the women who started and run the Motherless Daughters Organization. Many grievers find medical, social, or political causes that give form to their pain, providing a voice for that which is unspeakable and a harness for that which is unbridled.

Beverly is the woman who lost her thirty-three-year-old daughter Iris to AIDS nearly five years ago. Since then, Beverly has made AIDS her cause. She told me,

> I work in a restaurant in a community that is sheltered from the reality of AIDS. I wear a red ribbon; I put signs up; I ram it down their throats. It's my cause now. I mean, I have no other place. When I try to be in the other world, I don't belong there. I can be in the

other world for a little while—you know, nonsense, small talk—but my world is too serious. I'm in the world of dying and people know that. Sometimes people will call me and say can you help? I'm an oasis for certain people in that area, and I will direct them. My name is known in the AIDS community; they know they can call on me.

Beverly's name certainly is known in that community for a number of reasons. First, Beverly started an ongoing support group for bereaved mothers. Finding that she no longer fit into a group for mothers of persons with AIDS, she contacted other mothers from that group whose children had died and she told them, "We're starting a group, we'll run it ourselves, we don't need anybody to run the groups for us." She says, "We're each in different stages of grief but we understand. There's a core of us that meet twice a month, and this is a group that's never going to stop. It's an ongoing thing."

Beverly also started a hotline for bereaved mothers as well as the Mother's March Against AIDS.

When I started organizing the Mother's March, everybody said don't do it; you can't do it; you shouldn't do it; it's too much; it's not going to work; nobody's going to come. The more they said that, the more I was determined. What got me angry enough was one politician—I was talking about AIDS to him and he didn't know that I lost a child to AIDS, and he said, "Why are you worried about AIDS, only certain people get AIDS, it doesn't affect you." And this was a very intelligent politician. I thought, you know something, if this man thinks this way, then the whole country must think this way. So I said it's time for the people in this world to see the face of AIDS.

So Beverly organized; she drummed up support. She got media attention, and they had 1,100 marchers in Washington, D.C., for the first annual Mother's March Against AIDS in 1994. Every year the march grows bigger.

Certainly one of the reasons that Beverly does this work is because she wants to help others.

One of my motivations is to help other mothers and to help people, to stop AIDS, to get a cure. I cannot help my daughter anymore, but maybe seeing what we're going through may be appealing to the powers that be. Maybe they'll push for a cure faster. It's trying to save the next generation. I don't want other mothers to be in the pain that I'm in. I don't want it. I don't want any more mothers in my group. Knowing that I was a help to somebody, it gives you a purpose; it really gives you a purpose.

But Outreach is not the only motivation for this type of work. That is why Reinvestment in a cause is ultimately different and distinct from Outreach. The primary reason for Reinvestment in a cause is because it keeps the griever alive through giving them something productive to do. When I asked Beverly, "Why do you do this?" She said, "I think if I stopped, I would probably die." Beverly does this because it gives her life meaning, structure, purpose. Beverly invests in this cause now to keep herself alive.

I'm living the only way I can. I don't know where else I'd be. I can't say, "Okay, my life was rudely interrupted by my daughter's death, let me go back to where I was before that"—it doesn't work that way. I'm not the same person; I'm changed. You can't see AIDS, and live with it, and come out of it the same person. It's a slow, torturous, painful death that you watch your child go through every day. I would lay in bed and pray that it wouldn't be too bad for her and she could make it through the day. It was horrible for a mother to see. You die with them, a piece of you dies with them. You don't come out of that and say let me go back to what I was before, because you are not what you were before. Don't even try it; it's never going to work. So you better find another place for yourself. And that's it, that's what we're doing with the group, the hotline, the march.

Beverly's response to Synthesis, the lifelong stage of integrating loss into life, is to reinvest in a cause that gives her life meaning and keeps her motivated. Reinvestment in a cause is motivated by the need to channel energy and pain, funneling it into an activity that is personally meaningful. By doing this, one refuels a parched spirit, and the by-product is that one also helps others who suffer.

Reinvestment in a Creative Project

Another way of channeling energy in a healing way is to harness the creative spirit through visual, musical, and written arts. The arts offer a wide range of possibility in providing an avenue for creative investment. You may remember that Suse, whose son was killed in Pan Am 103, is a sculptor who uses her professional skills to give expression to the horror of losing a child. She began by expressing her own pain through a visual medium, then she reached out to others who had also lost their loved ones in the Pan Am crash. "Then it dawned on me, I didn't have to express all the different emotions of what happens to a mother. Let them come and portray their own feelings and in the end, I'll have them all. I'll engulf all the different feelings. And that's what happened."

Suse has each woman come to her studio with a picture of her loved one, which she tapes onto a wall with all the other happy, smiling faces of people killed in that flight. The woman then stands on a platform while Suse talks to her, gently guiding her to the moment when she heard of the flight's fate. Each woman reenacts her moment of anguish and horror, with limbs bent over, arms raised, hands clasped, and legs buckled. Some are screaming. Some are in a heap. Some clutch their stomachs.

Suse said when she connects with these other mothers in her studio, it is an incredibilbly special moment.

When I have a mother here who shares her most horrible moment in life with me, I feel incredibly privileged and I feel like I want to whisper. I don't want to intrude. It's a very special moment that is really holy to me. It brings us so together.

People ask me if it brings back my own pain. I say of course, but, you see, I don't mind that, because it's always there anyway. What people seem to think is that it goes away and that when another woman shares this with me, it brings it back. Well, it never goes away so it can never be brought back because it's always there.

The figures are made of a hollow welded steel frame covered with wire mesh, synthetic stone, and fiberglass and are painted in earth-tone hues. Suse devised this procedure because of its weather-resistant properties and its affordability. Each figure weighs approximately two hundred pounds, giving each piece weight and substance. Inside each figure, close to the heart, she includes an object or trinket of the deceased, making each piece truly unique and truly personalized. She has completed almost 30 larger-than-life-sized figures out of a planned total of 125, thus making this project essentially her life's work.

The figures are displayed together in outdoor public spaces as an exhibit entitled "Dark Elegy," which is both a memorial to those who died in Pan Am 103 and a testimony to all victims of terrorism. A plaque describing the work reads in part, "I want it to remind ourselves that life is fragile and that we can lose that which is most precious to us in an instant and have to live with that for the remainder of our lives."

But while this work affects the many hundreds of viewers who see it, and while it profoundly affects the many women who are involved, Suse's primary goal was not to help others. She started this project to help herself, to channel her rage and pain, and for her son Alexander to live on. She told me,

I do it because I need to do it. I'm very selfish. I think it's great if it in turn helps other people, but it somehow is not part at all of why I'm doing it. It's a terrific thing that it goes beyond my own satisfaction, but that is not why I do it.

When you have someone die that you loved very, very, very much, you want him or her remembered. You want them to somehow live on in memory. That is what "Dark Elegy" does. That is why the women involved feel positive about it. Because somehow their loved ones live on, by the piece speaking for itself. There is something that remains with the artwork. I think one of the reasons why the women respond so positively to the project is because there is something that remains that keeps something alive, that makes a statement for long after we are gone.

Music is another powerful means of expression that touches all who hear it. After his two-year-old son died due to an accidental fall from a window, one of Eric Clapton's responses was to write the beautiful and poignant song "Tears in Heaven." This song has touched millions of people who continue to hear it and respond to its message.

I was once deeply affected by a similar kind of creative and musical expression of grief when I was a member of a large metropolitan chorus and we sang a song commissioned by a bereaved father; the music was composed by a bereaved father, set to the text of a poem written by a bereaved father, and ultimately conducted by a bereaved father. This collaboration resulted in a performance of such exquisite, haunting beauty . . . suffice it to say that no one left that concert unmoved. This too was an example of Reinvestment.

It isn't necessary to creatively invest on a professional level. The goal is to harness your energy into something creative and productive on whatever level. A bereaved mother in Nantucket began a garden after her daughter committed suicide. She said, "I can't tell you why or how, one just comes to these things—I found that digging seemed to help." She continued, "It was one of those things you think of as being a mindless activity, but actually it was more than mindless. In fact it was just the opposite, because my mind was doing the digging. Not in any conscious way; I didn't even understand what was happening." What this griever experienced is that her mind became totally engaged and focused on her activity. The gardening, in a sense, absorbed her grief and gave her a creative outlet to channel her need to nurture and create. The garden got bigger and bigger until a quarter acre of land became more garden and less grass, until it became a profusion of color and life, a living legacy to her daughter.

Barbara's Story

We can't end our discussion of Reinvestment until we look at Barbara, our SOAR traveler, to see how she navigated this pathway. We know that after the death of her brother Bobby she descended into "chaos." She said, "Everything about grief is chaos. Grief is an insanity, really. Other societies, other cultures understand it and give it the respect that insanity is due. It's an experience out of reason, out of time and space." But Barbara survived this chaos and ultimately followed the pathways toward Transcendence. She traveled the pathway of Spirituality—for her it meant rediscovering her Christian roots and developing a richer, deeper faith. She traveled the pathway of Outreach—for her it meant volunteering in the AIDS community and later starting her Sisters support groups. She traveled the pathway of

Attitude—for her it meant acknowledging and embracing the gifts that flowed from grief. And now she travels the pathway of Reinvestment—for her it meant writing her beautiful and poetic memoir about her brother's death, *Landscape Without Gravity*.

After Bobby died, I was trying to think what to do for my next book. [Barbara is a writer by profession.] I tried a novel, but that didn't work. I tried a lot of other, different subjects. I was sitting around and suddenly I thought I've got to write about Bobby. Then I thought no, that's the last thing I want to write about. And I fought it and fought it and fought it. The only way I had the courage to do it since it obviously had to be written, was that first I would go to the chapel at my church every morning—I would go there to cry first before I went to write. And then I would go to the library where I would be surrounded by people, because I thought I'll be with other people and if I become raving mad since I'm going deep into the pain in this book, if I become a raving lunatic, these people will take me to the hospital. So I wrote the book longhand at the library, and it was the only way I dared to do it. Those people will never know what they would have been called upon to do if necessary.

Barbara wrote the book because, first and foremost, she needed to write it for herself, to channel her energy in that way. But Barbara's example of Reinvestment overlaps with Outreach since ultimately she realized that her book would help other grievers.

The other sign that I had to write the book was that I'd written a short essay for the magazine section of the *Times* and had gotten a huge amount of mail about it. And that was the first I heard that people don't talk about grief. Letters said, "Nobody ever talks about this," or "You put my feelings into words." Hundreds and hundreds of letters like this. So I started thinking maybe it really does have to be a book.

People would say, "I lost a friend and nobody understands." They all felt that they were alone. So much of what I did after Bobby died was that I didn't want people to be alone. I started wearing a red ribbon at all times because I thought if I'd ever seen one while Bobby was sick, I would have felt so much less alone. The book sort of became exactly what I dreamed that it would become, which is the hand to hold other hands.

Barbara's book, then, served not only as a means of working through her own grief, but also as a bridge to other bereaved siblings, to other grievers in general so that they weren't alone anymore. Reinvestment in a creative project exorcises the pain and exercises the creative force, which ultimately is a link back to life. Furthermore, by transcending the self and engaging in something larger than the self, there is a deep, heartfelt return to the land of the living.

Reinvestment over Time

Some grievers will choose to always be involved with causes that are related to their grief. Other grievers will do it for a time and then later move on to other projects. Transcendence is fluid and reinvestments change over time. For Barbara, now that she has written her book for and about Bobby, her next mission is to move on to something else. Barbara said,

When I came up for the idea for the new book [the history of romance], it was very clear to me that Bobby said, "You've done this, now do something happy." And the idea for this book just came out of nowhere. And of course it is an idea that makes me happy. It just makes me happy all the time. With that came a sense truly of his moving on. He died in 1989. This happened to me in the spring of 1995—and it was a physical sensation as well as a spiritual sensation, a physical lightening and a spiritual lightening. I absolutely feel that he stuck around and helped me out as long as I needed it. I felt very much that he was helping me because I was in such terrible, terrible pain. He was helping me out of the pain, and I just sort of followed.

So reinvestments change over time. And their goals and purposes change over time. Sometimes they are motivated by the desire to help others, and at other times, they are motivated by the need to help the self. But what is consistent and critical in defining and understanding reinvestments as a means to Transcendence is that they are about channeling the pain and energy stimulated by the loss into something meaningful and productive.

SOAR as a Bridge to Life

We've now looked at each of the four pathways toward Transcendence: Spirituality, Outreach, Attitude, and Reinvestment. The pathways are dynamic and fluid. They change over time; they evolve; they flow into one another. Ultimately each pathway is about change as a response to Synthesis. Knowing that life cannot ever be the same, the pathways are about changing in a positive way. They build a bridge back to life—a different life, to be sure—but life nevertheless.

But what happens if the bridge is suddenly cluttered with tollbooths and locked gates? What happens if the bridge cannot be crossed because you are dragging too much heavy baggage to travel? In part 4 we look at some of the obstacles that prevent people from transcending, for many people are overwhelmed by their losses and get stuck in the mire of bitterness and grief. The next few chapters will look at these problems, with suggestions for getting back on track.

PART IV

Roadblocks and Detours to Transcendence

CHAPTER 10

Spiritual Doubt and Conflict

Grief drives men into the habits of serious reflection, sharpens the understanding and softens the heart.
—JOHN ADAMS

In Gabriel García Márquez's whimsical novel *Of Love and Other Demons*, a marquis loses his faith in God as a result of having witnessed his wife struck dead by lightning. As we know from chapter 6, doubt and spiritual confusion are normal, often necessary, experiences in the grieving process. However, not everyone works through the process to a state of faith reconstruction. The marquis in this novel, since his wife's death, has been unable to restore or rebuild his faith. Many years later, after his daughter is bitten by a rabid dog, he speaks with a bishop concerning his lost faith. The bishop is not at all surprised by the marquis's lack of belief. In fact, he says he too lost his faith when he was a twenty-one-year-old soldier engaged in battle.

"It was the thundering certainty that God had ceased to exist," he said. In terror he had dedicated himself to a life of prayer and penitence.

"Until God took pity on me and showed me the path of my vocation," he concluded. "What is essential, therefore, is not that you no longer believe, but that God continues to believe in you. And regarding that there can be no doubt, for it is He in His infinite diligence who has enlightened us so that we may offer you this consolation."

The bishop worked through his own loss of faith and now assures the marquis that God has not, in fact, turned His back but has even led the marquis to those who can provide assistance.

There is no question that working through the profound spiritual issues and questions that grief ignites is arduous, often discouraging work. Some grievers get so lost on the journey that they reject their long-held beliefs and seek new ones. Others, feeling victimized by religious institutions, reject the pathway completely. And still others merely remain stuck, mired in their spiritual doubts and anger. Whatever the particular circumstance, it is, for many people, a devastating double blow to lose one's faith as well as one's beloved.

This chapter will look at different types of religious and spiritual dysfunction—religion being the organized, formal institution and spirituality being the private, inner connection with the Divine. This chapter will also look at some solutions. I certainly don't have all the answers, and I cannot tell you what to believe; spirituality is an intensely private and personal issue. But I will share with you several examples of how other grievers have navigated the treacherous passages in their own individual ways. The goal is to redefine a sense of faith, however different it might be from the predeath faith, and to establish a new relationship with the Divine, whatever this term may mean to an individual. The end result is often a richer belief system that can lead one to Transcendence.

Being Angry with God

It has been fifteen years since Sara's father died. If you ask her about her father's death, she immediately says, "How could a loving God watch my father suffer such a painful death?" She told me, "Before my father died, he too questioned God's ways and wondered why he had to suffer. But eventually he believed again and found his faith comforting in the end." She continued, "I couldn't buy it, though. I saw my father waste away in pain. I said to myself, there cannot be a merciful God if this can happen." Sara watched her father die, became angry and confused, but then remained stuck. She didn't try to work through any process of faith. She was left with empty, bitter feelings toward God that have lasted fifteen years. To this day, this previously devout woman no longer has faith. When she discusses this loss, there is pain in her eyes.

For many people, one of the biggest stumbling blocks and one of the biggest traps for getting stuck is the entire concept of being angry with God. First you have to admit the anger, then you have to sit with the anger, and finally, you have to release the anger.

Granted, being angry at God is a pretty loaded issue. Many of us grew up believing that anger toward God was downright blasphemous. So rather than stir up the guilt that would result from impolite, unholy accusations toward God, many of us hold our rage inside. And there it smolders. So the first task of coping with this anger is to freely, nonjudgmentally acknowledge it.

Contrary to whatever many of us have read or been told, I believe it's okay to be angry at God. God can take it. Just as the parent of a toddler can sustain the temper tantrums of his child and the parent of an adolescent learns to tolerate the rageful outbursts of his teenager, so too does God accept and permit our rageful tantrums.

Once you've acknowledged the anger, you have to sit with it. In one of my bereavement groups, a woman whose father had died was sharing with the group that she couldn't bring herself to recite Kaddish (the traditional Jewish mourner's prayer) for her father. She shared that she was just too angry to pray in any way. When I asked her how she felt about not being able to pray the Kaddish in synagogue, she responded, "Oh, I'm not worried. I know I'll be able to again one day, but for now I'm just too darn mad and I guess I just have to stay with that." This woman no doubt will work it through because she's respecting and accepting of the process and the need to stay with the anger.

For many people, just acknowledging it, accepting it, expressing it, and sitting with it is enough to get the anger moving. For others, it requires an active campaign of talking with others and sifting through information. For some, that means talking with ministers and rabbis, trying different church communities, and consciously reworking a faith. It's a struggle, to be sure, but the reward is a renewed sense of spirituality.

Working through the Anger

Ten years ago, at the age of twenty-nine, Martha had just moved to a new community with her second husband, her five-year-old son from a previous marriage, and her six-week-old newborn. One day, Martha came home after taking her son to kindergarten in the morning to find her husband dead in their bedroom. He had committed suicide by hanging himself with a belt in their closet.

Martha's husband had a history of depression and had, in fact, been acting strangely the past few days. But he had been elated at the birth of their baby, and Martha had no reason to suspect the deadly, self-destructive thoughts that were going on in his mind. She said, "When I saw him, it was like lightning struck me. It was a physical sensation, it just hit me and it traveled through my body, like a bolt, through my feet into the floor—that's what it felt like. It was a complete physical shock."

Martha said that after his death, everything was broken and shattered in her life, including her faith. "From the minute my husband died, I felt it marked me. Like I stood on the earth and walked on the earth in a different way than ever before." She remembers feeling guilty and bitter for at least seven years, but she kept living for her children's sakes. And now she's a deeply religious woman. I asked her about her anger and her faith.

At first I thought, "Why did God allow this to happen?" And then for years and years, I felt very angry at God. My faith went from being superficial to being nonexistent. Faith! Faith in what? After some point I felt like I couldn't do it anymore, and in some moments of desperation I recall praying to God for strength. I would say, "If you can't do anything else for me, at least give me strength to go on and get these kids grown, and give them a decent lifestyle," and it has been hard.

It sort of started that way, and then I just started feeling led to people. I met a Chinese psychologist who taught me about acupressure and tai chi exercise. He said to me, "Ultimately any work you do with the body is for the purpose of allowing spiritual growth, because it can't happen unless the body is open."

I started attending a Quaker worship service. I was seeking, well, it was really a way of finding a community. They believe that God is in all of us, and that we must listen to the voice within. They worship in silence together; they listen. They seemed to be very centered and peaceful people.

Then I moved and I started attending a Lutheran congregation there, and I began addressing my standing in relation to God and the issue of God's existence. For a long time, I realized, I was very angry at God, that God had ceased to exist to me as a beneficent, paternal, loving figure. I had to come to grips with that and let go of some things.

I asked her how she did that and what helped her on her journey of seeking and questioning and letting go of anger.

It helped me to talk to a minister. He set me on the way to another minister, the one I have now, who is very easy to talk to. His wife has cancer and he's had to deal with the anticipation of the loss of his wife, and why would God do that. It's hard to articulate how it becomes apparent that suffering through things opens one's eyes to an understanding of life, and one's spiritual existence in a different way.

Martha rebuilt her religious community and her spiritual life. She did this by consciously, actively searching. She tried the Quaker faith, the Lutheran tradition. She met with ministers. She consulted a Chinese doctor. She actively allowed herself to engage in the process of redefining her faith and her God. She allowed herself to be angry with God. And through her anger and doubts, she eventually redefined her image of God and her relationship with Him.

As time passed, I could see it was almost as if I had been carried through. Sometimes I don't know how I did it; I couldn't have done it on my own—it was too enormous. Then I started to believe and just think about God a lot differently, that He can act in our life in specific ways, but He's not going to shield us from that which is human and can and does happen to all humans. I started thinking about the nature of humanity, and how that is life—I could walk out now and be hit by a truck and that's it—will God save me from that? Not necessarily, but can I get strength, can I lean on Him? It seems to be able to happen.

Martha's commentary on her evolved belief in God made me think of a beautiful poem called "Footprints."

I dreamed I was walking along the beach with the Lord,
and across the sky flashed scenes from my life.
For each scene, I noticed two sets of footprints in the sand,
one belonged to me, the other to the Lord.
When the last scene of my life flashed before us
I looked back at the footprints in the sand.
I noticed that many times along the path of my life,
there was only one set of footprints.
I also noticed that it happened at the very lowest and
saddest times in my life.
I questioned the Lord about it.
"Lord, You said that once I decided to follow You,
You would walk with me all the way.
But I have noticed that during the most troublesome times,
there is only one set of footprints.
I don't understand why in times when I need You most,
You would leave."
The Lord replied, "My precious child, I would never leave
you during your times of trial and suffering.
When you see only one set of footprints,
it was then that I carried you."

—Anonymous

In the end, Martha didn't find her faith restored, she found it redefined. Once the anger had lifted, and Martha was able to sift through her feelings about God, she realized concepts she previously held dear no longer made sense. Ideas she had believed about God didn't seem accurate. The belief system that no longer worked had to be replaced by one that made sense to Martha. To do this, she had to be willing to rethink all that she believed about God.

Rethinking God

Rethinking God involves an active internal and external journey of questioning, reflecting, and meditating. It involves change and new ideas. Basically you have to look at the old image, possibly let it go, and create a new one.

Michael is a griever whom I mentioned in chapter 7 whose twenty-year-old brother was brutally murdered fifteen years ago. Michael also questioned God's ways and realized that he needed to come up with a new image of God. Here are his thoughts on the spiritual journey that he underwent after this tragedy:

After Alex died, it changed my view of God a lot. There really couldn't be a God the way I was taught there's a God, because what happened, that's just too much—that's outside the margins that I have of what "Oz the Great and Powerful" would allow. I had to renegotiate that whole idea, because clearly God isn't, you know, God isn't Father Time. He's not this cute old guy, this Walt Disney portrait. Other than the story of Job, the issue of bad things happening to people isn't really addressed in the Bible. Silence is what we've been left with. But I knew my ideas were bunk when Alex was killed because no way could the Walt Disney God allow something like that to happen. That made me figure out, maybe that God isn't real.

I went through a period where I tried on the "life without a God" concept. It doesn't really work. You have to have some faith in some kind of order, at least I think. Even faith in the disorder, because in the end there is no order and you must be able to trust the disorder. Without faith, you really have nothing. Faith is to ourselves the way a playpen is to a child. It's a context in which you can survive.

Michael had to let go of an old image before he could redefine a new one. He worked through a process of faith and arrived at a deeper level of peace. Allowing the process to unfold is key. But doing so is understandably frightening because once you start reexamining God and your faith, you may find yourself facing a lot more questions than answers.

In other words, as you tear down the foundation and begin renovation on your model of how the world works, you may discover that the new model isn't as simple or as blindly secure. The new structure may even have some holes and uncertainties in it. But if you let it, it can ultimately result in a richer textured faith.

I told you about Jim who created the New England Center for Loss and Transition in response to his wife's unexpected death. Jim was a very religious man, so when his wife so tragically and unexpectedly died, he understandably went through a terrible time with his faith. He told me that his whole spirituality, his relationship with God, was transformed.

My vision and perception of God changed radically after this event. I always perceived God to be someone that takes care of the just, the fair, and the good. If you do good, you will have good done to you. If it wasn't stated that way, it certainly was envisioned that way. And when this [his wife's death] happened, it turned that assumption around, and I said, "This really stinks.

What am I doing all the good for? Why be righteous and good if there's no reward at the end?" You ask all those questions. I was angry at God, angry at myself for being naive in my theology.

It changed my focus and my image of God as one who takes care of to one who struggles with you, one who walks with you in your pain and who walks with you when you struggle. My prayer is reformed now, much less with words and much more with actions. What I do with this center is my prayer.

My whole concept of an afterlife has changed. I always believed it was some kind of beneficent, magnificent, paradisial experience, that when you die you are welcomed into the arms of a welcoming God. And you'll be happy for the rest of your life in this other state, whatever it is. And now? . . . I don't have a clue. It is just so incredibly ambiguous. I hope there's an afterlife, part of me believes in that, but clearly you can't prove it. You can't prove heaven, you can't prove an afterlife. You base it on nothing but faith, which is really hope.

I asked Jim if he experienced this loss of pure, innocent, "naive" faith as a significant loss to his life.

It feels like a loss, yes, and I struggle with that all the time. I have less confidence in faith now than I did before. But maybe I'm more real because of that. I certainly feel a lot more honest now than I did before. At least now I'm asking real questions and saying, "What do you *really* believe?" My faith is a source of confusion, and it's not as secure and it's not as comfortable, absolutely . . . but I am convinced and I've always said—I've just never lived it—I've always said that good spirituality is struggle. It's struggling with questions. It's the dark night of the soul. Things become a little clearer as you move on with the struggle. That's one of the things that has come back, because it's been reworked, in a new image, the hope that there is a God, the belief that there is a God.

Jim explained to me that it was the very loss of his faith, the very need to redefine his beliefs, that brought about a richer, deeper, albeit more confusing, spirituality.

It was a great experience theologically, spiritually, because I wrestled with a lot of questions, and still do. That's really what good spirituality does—it's not having the answers but having better and better questions. And I'm back on that track again. I had the conclusions before. That was dangerous. The conclusion now is that there are very few conclusions, but I'm more open to that now.

The spiritual struggle requires being open to redefining God, rethinking theology, and reexamining faith. What may result are a lot more questions than answers, but as Jim says, that's what good theology is, and that's when a leap of faith is required in its purest sense. Some questions you may solve, and others might never be answered, so faith means tolerating the uncertainties while still connecting with your God.

Religious Obstacles

Unfortunately, what some people find is that just as they are embarking on this tremendous spiritual journey, just as they are struggling with the deepest questions, organized religions the very institutions that should be offering support for the sojourn—make the journey more difficult still. Religions may actually exacerbate the spiritual pain by squelching the search and by force-feeding solutions.

Not all religions like uncertainty. Many religions prefer to offer the solutions. Sometimes, in the name of having the answers, religions subtly ask you not to feel. Consolers and grievers alike often say or think things like, "God must have needed her more than I did," or "My child is in heaven now with the Lord." I have heard grievers berating themselves that if they only trusted God more, they wouldn't feel so badly. Or that they should be happy because their loved one is in heaven now. I have even heard of clergy who have urged grievers to be thankful for the will of God and to rejoice that their loved ones are with the Lord. The danger with these thoughts is that they may short-circuit grief; they might prematurely block the necessary grieving process. Religion becomes problematic when it asks you not to hurt, not to feel bad, not to fully experience the feelings of Disorganization. Yes, your beloved may be in heaven now, but you still have to face the pain and anguish of the loss. There are no shortcuts, not even spiritual ones.

Many grievers end up feeling revictimized by their religious community when they are told to give thanks for "God's will" rather than allowed to feel angry and sad for their loss. The concept of God's will is difficult at best, a classic double-edged sword. On the one hand, though we may not understand or agree with God's will, believing in it as a concept brings comfort. On the other hand, believing in God's will is not so much comforting as it is terrifying. If a tragedy reflects God's will, then our loved one's death could be viewed as a personal punishment.

The nineteenth-century Norwegian playwright Henrik Ibsen captured this idea in *The Master Builder* when a character, Mrs. Solness, talks about having her twin sons die.

HILDE (*softly*): You lost the two little boys.

MRS. SOLNESS: Ah yes. Them. Well, you see *that* was a different kind of thing. That was the will of the Lord. And one must submit to a thing like that. And give thanks, too.

HILDE: Do you?

MRS. SOLNESS: Not always. I'm afraid. I know quite well that it's my duty. But I *can't* do it, all the same.

HILDE: No, no, that's only natural, I think.

MRS. SOLNESS: And time and again I have to say to myself, that it was a just punishment for me—

HILDE: Why?

MRS. SOLNESS: Because I wasn't steadfast enough in misfortune.

HILDE: But I don't see that—

MRS. SOLNESS: Oh no, no, Miss Wangel. Don't talk to me any more about the two little boys. We must only be glad for them. For everything's well with them—all's well now.

Mrs. Solness uses her beliefs to short-circuit her grief ("We must only be glad for them") rather than face her loss. But this belief also implies that the death of her sons was God's way of punishing her for something she did wrong. Such beliefs can cause tremendous guilt and unnecessary self-flagellation on top of all the pain the griever is suffering.

One result of this confusion and guilt is that often grievers first turn their backs on religion and then turn their backs on God. Eva is the twenty-six-year-old woman discussed in chapter 9 whose brother was murdered ten years ago. She told me,

> I do respect and believe in God's will but it wasn't helpful to hear that after Bruce was killed. Actually, this turned me away from the church. [She begins to cry]. I grew up Catholic and went to Catholic schools most of my life. I felt that I led a Christian life, but when this happened it was devastating. You feel like if you lead a good life and you're a good person, then nothing bad will happen to you . . . and then something does and everything is shattered. So, I hated God and I hated the church. I felt there was no God, no justice. In the last few years, I've been able to go to church, but I don't go regularly and when I go, it's very emotional. My brother's gone and I should be praying for him every day. What if he's suffering in purgatory and I'm not helping him? [She cries harder.] I'm ashamed of my spiritual weakness.

Eva is still struggling. She's burdened by guilt, by religious obstacles that make her feel weak. When beliefs cast blame, when they cause pain, when they invite guilt and distress, it may be time to reevaluate them.

Sometimes it's the religious institutions themselves that foster these feelings of guilt and blame. "Controversial" deaths are condemned by some religions: death by abortion, suicide, AIDS. The result is that some grievers are alienated by the very communities who should be providing support.

Reverend Jimmy Allen is a Baptist preacher and the former head of the sixteen-million-member Southern Baptist Convention. He is by all accounts a wise, helpful, and compassionate man. His son Scott, also a preacher, married Lydia, a pediatric nurse. In 1982, when Lydia was seven months pregnant, she went into toxic shock and needed a blood transfusion. Two months later, Lydia gave birth to Matthew, and three years later, she gave birth to Bryan.

In 1985 they discovered that the blood had been tainted by the AIDS virus. Lydia and the two children were infected. Over the course of the next ten years, Bryan died, Lydia died, and finally, Matthew died. Scott lost his wife and two sons. Jimmy lost his daughter-in-law and two grandsons.

Burden of a Secret is Jimmy's book that chronicles the sad and painful experience that he had when his church turned its back on him and his family in their hours of need. Why? Because of the AIDS virus and all the unholy prejudice against it. Scott was fired from his job as minister of education in a church. Jimmy was rebuffed by the church that he had loved and led. The book is about a preacher's disillusionment and a family's anguish. Jimmy Allen lost three beloved family members, and he lost his church.

Some people, either by choice or by chance, lose their church. Others, as we have discussed, lose their spiritual connection with and understanding of God. Either or both losses on top of the loss of your beloved may deal a lethal blow to the underpinnings of your entire philosophical system. Reworking your beliefs, your concept of God, your relationship with God, and your relationship with a church demands active, conscious attention.

The purpose of religion is to be a vehicle, an avenue of facilitating spiritual connections with the Divine. And yet, as we've seen, many people find that religion isn't so much a helpful bridge to spirituality as a gated tollbooth with padlock and chains. In rethinking how to unlock the gate and restore free transportation, some people find that they choose to abandon their childhood religions. They choose to go on a search for a new faith community that can support rather than condemn, that can nourish rather than diminish, that can sustain rather than victimize.

Others find that they remain within a religious context but need to reinterpret doctrine and scripture. After Sylvia's twenty-six-year-old son committed suicide, a sin in the eyes of the Catholic church, she felt haunted by the thought that her son was stuck in purgatory. She told me that she went from priest to priest searching for assurance that he wasn't in hell, that he was at peace, and that she would see him again. She was eventually told that God forgives those who are sick and that mental illness is a sickness. So, overturning a belief that she had been raised on, she was able to put her fears to rest. Her religion ultimately became a cornerstone in her ability to cope with her son's death.

A Spiritual Journey

Let's look at Victoria and how she coped after her husband was killed in a car accident. Victoria is the widow we met in chapter 9 who took the pathway of Reinvestment by reinvesting in a second marriage. She also ultimately took the pathway of Spirituality as well, but not without a great deal of struggle and strife. Victoria went on an extensive external and internal journey to reestablish her faith and renew her relationship with God.

In 1983, Victoria was in the midst of a busy life as a wife and a mother. She and her husband, Bill, had an eleven-year-old son and a thirteen-year-old daughter and they had recently moved to a new community. Over New Year's weekend, they went with two other couples and their children for a skiing vacation in New England.

On New Year's Eve, in the early afternoon, Bill left the ski lodge, saying, "I'll see you back at the house at 3:30." When Victoria got back to the house with the children, there was no Bill. She continues:

All the people I was with said, "Oh, Victoria, why are you so nervous? He's just gone out for a drive, a newspaper." I thought, no, Bill was the kind of person who was always where he said he was going to be. If he said he was going to be there when I got home from skiing, then I knew he'd be there. Much to everybody else's consternation, I took a shower and then in half an hour, at 4:00 P.M., I was on the phone to the police, which everyone else thought was ridiculous.

I said, "I'm Mrs. Jones, and I know it's kind of silly to be asking, because my husband's only been missing half an hour, but do you have any record of a Bill Jones?" And they said, "Let us have someone call you back right away." I said, "Fine." I assumed that I had gotten the emergency number and I was taking their time and that they were going to have someone routine call me back. So instead, the phone rang a few minutes later and it was the county medical examiner, and he said, "Mrs. Jones, we have a Mr. Bill Jones here and he has expired." I said, "What? I don't believe you, how dare you, who are you to tell me such a thing, how dare you?" It was so out of anywhere that I couldn't comprehend what he was saying.

Then he said, "Would you come to the funeral home and identify him?" And I said yes, I would. I guess I was almost yelling into the phone, I guess my children and everybody heard me on the phone. So my children came over to me, and I just said to them, "Your father's dead," because that was the fact. They both burst into tears, and I remember each of the mothers took a child into their lap and hugged them and held onto them. Then one of the fathers drove me to the funeral home.

Victoria and her children were hit with the most unimaginable punch that life can deliver—that someone you love can be killed instantly, with zero preparation and no time for goodbyes. With a blow this extreme and unexpected, it can literally take months and months for the reality of the loss to sink in.

I remember thinking that once Bill died, it was like all four walls of my house had come down. The world I knew absolutely changed overnight. I never would have believed that the world could change overnight, I just never believed it. It would have been an incomprehensible thought to me if I had not lived through it, that every single relationship could change, the way every single person perceived me and talked to me and related to me could change. That my view on almost everything could change overnight. I just would never believe it possible. But that's what happened.

As Victoria and her children went through the stages of Disorganization and Reconstruction, Victoria found herself going on a spiritual and religious journey. Her journey began, interestingly, upon seeing the body of her dead husband in the funeral home.

I went in and Bill was on a platform thing covered up head to toe by a blanket. I looked and said yes, that was Bill. Something possessed me—I don't know what it was—to push his eyes back open. I pushed them back and there was the most wonderful look in his eyes. I'll never forget it. At the time, the only image that came to me was my religious image. Bill was a very devout Catholic, wore crosses underneath his shirt. He was very traditional and old-fashioned in his Catholicism. At the time, I thought he must have met the Lord, he must have met the spirit, because there was such an incredible joy and wonder, radiance in his eyes. I just looked at him and thought, whatever happened to this person, look at his eyes—it was joyful and radiant and a sense of wonder. It was unbelievable. So I closed his eyes and kissed him goodbye.

Victoria had a history of being religious herself. She said, "For years and years I had gone to church, to Bible studies. I went to Bible studies with groups of other young mothers. And they sustained me; it was really my source of encouragement and support and wisdom and insight that gave me a lot of what I needed to get through the years of being married and a young mother. But when Bill was killed, everything that I had learned, or the things that I had most treasured in the Bible, no longer applied to me. They were just no longer applicable, they were irrelevant. Or they were wrong."

Victoria realized that what she had believed in no longer held true. And she was angry . . . angry at God.

Our marriage had been based on some fairly conservative religious beliefs, the old gospel that "if you do your duty, if you're loyal, if you're faithful, if you are loving, somehow life will prosper you, God will take care of you." Yes, I was very angry that that hadn't happened. My daughter said it quite well, she said "Mother, God promised to take care of us, and he didn't." He hadn't. So I certainly couldn't listen anymore to anything about the providence of God, or the goodness of God. I couldn't even face going to church anymore.

Victoria subsequently experienced a profound sense of loss, not only of her husband but of everything that she had based her life on, her entire belief system.

It felt like this enormous vacuum. The loss of having a set of tenets by which to live your life, a set of core beliefs by which to sort of conduct your daily life, was very central to who I was as a young mother. And so to have all of that basically irrelevant was a tremendous loss.

But Victoria responded with a proactive stance. If she lost her belief system, then she was going to create a new one. She decided to go to seminary.

> What I did do was to enroll full-time into seminary, because the way I saw it was, my entire conceptual basis of who I was and what I thought about anything in life had been totally smashed. For fifteen years I'd made this lovely home, lovely little family, lovely little children, and a sledgehammer had come and taken fifteen years of work and just pounded it into nothing, so that there was nothing to show for it. That's what I thought.
>
> I had no idea what to think anymore, or what to believe anymore. I didn't have another set of ideas that structured my life. But what I did have, and I remember saying it so clearly at seminary, "I believe there's a way. I do have enough faith to believe there is a way for me. I know somewhere there's a path, I just don't know what it is."

Victoria spent three years in a graduate program at the seminary, looking for the answers that would put her world back together. What she found is that she had to feel the pain of her loss, she had to fully experience the stage of Disorganization.

> After surviving, getting through the funeral and the estate and settling the children, finally I had the leisure to *feel*. I was reading a lot of theory about pain and loss. I remember one professor saying to me, "Well Victoria, your job now is just to go home and cry every

day for an hour. That's your task in life, that's where you are in life, and that's what you have to do." I did.

I was lucky in finding some very fine pastoral ministers who could touch my pain instead of letting me run away from it. I had a fine preacher who came to me one day. They had just been preaching for Easter about the crucifixion of Christ and Christ saying, "My God, my God, why have you abandoned me on the cross?" And this preacher said to me, "Victoria, you know what they're talking about in there, don't you? You really know what that means." That anyone really knew how I felt—that I could relate with Christ on the cross, the sense of abandonment, the sense of total desolation, the sense of being alone—was a great comfort to me. The ability to know the pain, to articulate the pain. The ministers didn't come and cry with me, but they had the insight to articulate in a pastoral way. Their words could pierce into my defenses, could pierce into my heart, could pierce through to who I was in a way that ultimately was very healing.

My experience was one of union. What happened to me from these words was an experience within my soul of a companion, a spiritual companion in Christ. I was not alone anymore. That was what was so healing and so joyful, is that I knew I was not alone.

The terrifying thing for me, the most painful, had been that I was alone; no one understood. The community very quickly ceased to understand. Two years after, they expected me to be remarried, because they had gotten over the death in two years, and why hadn't I? And so, the growing sense of isolation from the community I needed the most, the growing sense that peo-

ple did not understand me . . . and then to find that
there was a place where I was understood, where I was
really known, was so healing.

In retrospect, there's a part of me that is deeply
grateful that I was in a place that could be touched. I
suspect that there are many people who sustain losses
and are not in contact with people who can touch their
loss and so they repress it and they live with it, but it's
never touched.

Victoria felt her pain, she allowed it to be touched, and
she experienced not only a sense of community in the seminary, but also a sense of union with Christ. For her, it meant
identifying her pain and her abandonment with that which
Christ expressed while on the cross. And in the end, she
found a new sense of spirituality, a new relationship with her
God.

I was converted to a new level of relationship with
the spirit. I was converted to a deeper connection to
myself, to God, to the universal spirit, and to a community. If grievers turn away and become bitter, what's
happened is that they haven't found the new relationship. I don't think you can survive without something
to hold onto. I had this faith that there was a way, there
was a path, I just had to find it.

Victoria accepted the fact that she had to rebuild her faith.
She actively went about doing this by going to seminary and
confronting the questions head on. She still doesn't have all
the answers, but as she told me later, "Seminary always said

that we are called to withstand, not to understand. I think that's what I've come to believe too."

It was not Victoria's intention to become a minister by profession, so after seminary, she earned a social work degree, and then went on for training in family therapy. She now works in a mental health facility helping people touch their own pain. She tells me, "The social work, the family therapy, this is a form of ministry. The psychiatrist at my clinic said to me, 'Victoria, this is a pretty constructive way to use your pain. If everybody used their pain in this way, the world would be a better place.' That made me happy."

Victoria, by working through her spiritual and religious questions, reclaimed spirituality as a pathway to Transcendence. Her attitude toward life and death fueled this journey. By reaching out via a helping profession, and ultimately by reinvesting in life and love again, she has traveled through the valley of the shadow and back into the light. Victoria's personal journey demanded a great deal of work, effort, and emotional stamina. Not everyone needs to attend seminary to conduct their search, but certainly one must be willing to travel the sometimes arduous path to Transcendence.

Reclaiming the Spirit

Struggling with spiritual loss and disorientation is, at times, devastating. And the complex spiritual journey, which should be facilitated by religious supports, is too often complicated by factors such as religious short-circuiting, guilt, blame, or condemnation. The temptation for many is to give up the fight. But giving up the spiritual and religious struggle results in a poverty of spirit that to many is just as devastating as the loss of the beloved.

Sometimes you have to "act as if," which means acting *as if* you still believe, acting *as if* there is a good God, acting until meaning can be restored and until you no longer have to act. Through this process, it is important to be willing to ask the difficult questions, to tolerate the absence of answers, to be angry at God, and to rethink all that you have known.

So I invite you to embrace the whole religious and spiritual process, to actively search and bravely question. I invite you to "take what you need and leave the rest." I invite you to be lost, and eventually to be found. A renewed spiritual life is well worth the fight since it can ultimately be the most powerful, the most meaningful, and the most transcendent of all the pathways.

CHAPTER 11

Complicated Grief: When Time Doesn't Heal

If you bring forth what is within you,
What you bring forth will save you.
If you do not bring forth what is within you,
What you do not bring forth will destroy you.
—GOSPEL OF ST. THOMAS

True or false: Time heals all wounds. FALSE. Contrary to what you've ever been told, time *alone* does not heal all wounds. Often that's why people get stuck—they think they can wait it out, that if enough time goes by, they will actually feel better. But not necessarily. I'm reminded of what my grandmother used to say about the expression "practice makes perfect" with regard to my piano lessons when I was a little girl. She would say that if you practice something incorrectly, then no amount of practice will make it perfect. At the most, you will have a perfectly imperfect rendition. Therefore, she would say, *"perfect* practice makes perfect." The same is also true for grief.

If you're not doing the necessary grief work of feeling, expressing, and processing, or if you're holding onto your grief and not moving on to new investments and relationships, then time alone will only exacerbate the problems. Unresolved grief gets buried under depression, anxiety, relationship problems, health problems, and substance abuse. Some people never seem to "feel" anything, but later become clinically depressed. Others get so stuck in their anger and rage that they become threatening or violent. And some hold onto fear so tightly and for so long that they are emotionally paralyzed and incapable of loving. The nongriever or the blocked griever may never even recognize the connection, but scratch below the surface, and the links become readily apparent.

In other words, it is the movement *through* each of the critical phases of Shock, Disorganization, Reconstruction, and Synthesis to Transcendence that is so important. If you get stuck in one, or if you skip one altogether, then there may be problems. In fact, depending on your circumstances, time without grief work can potentially be quite harmful to you and your quality of life. So it's not "Time heals all wounds" but "Time plus the grief work and the grief process heals wounds."

As we've discussed, grief is not a smooth and easy road and therefore getting stuck is an expected part of the process. Even temporarily skipping phases is normal. But when the intensity of the block becomes dangerous, or when the duration of the emotional clog or avoidance is extreme, then there is a problem.

Certainly an entire book could be (and several have been) devoted to the topic of complicated mourning. This chapter cannot look at each and every type of grief dysfunction, but it will look at a few of the major problems with suggestions for healing. The most common phase to skip is Disorganization because it is so painful and emotionally draining. For many people, the temptation is to avoid such an intense and agonizing phase. Other people actually get *stuck in* Disorganization, and skip the stage of Reconstruction. They fail to move on with life, getting blocked by any number of emotional barricades, such as pain, idealization, anger and guilt. The good news is that if grief can become complicated, it can also become *un*complicated. It's never too late to go through the process and discover healing.

Skipping Disorganization

This is without question the number one type of grief problem. After the shock, after the news has settled, you want to avoid the pain. Therefore, grief is delayed, postponed, inhibited, repressed, avoided, and denied. Society is just as averse to "unpleasant" feelings as you are, so it applauds your attempts to build a wall around your heart, shutting out all the messy grief. Friends and family collude with you in your attempt to mask every feeling and avoid any encounter with the true, acute grief. And as we discussed in the last chapter, even some religions encourage you to deny your painful feelings.

So you diligently avoid grief by throwing yourself into work and activities, so many that you barely have time to breathe, much less time to stop and think or feel anything. You run like mad to avoid any sort of "breakdown." You tell everyone that you are "fine, just fine" when they ask, and they seem relieved that you are apparently "over it." They marvel at your strength and praise your resilience. And you keep the painful feelings—the anger, rage, sadness, depression, fear, anxiety, despair—deeply buried under thick layers of denial and defense.

Certainly everyone does this to a certain extent. And for many, there are some very compelling reasons to postpone grief (like a widow who has to rally to raise her young children). However, if the postponement goes on indefinitely, there will be negative consequences. The Disorganization-avoider may think she's outwitted the bitter pill of loss, but if she thinks she's escaped unscathed, she's wrong. Chances are she may be fearful, cynical, hardened. She may feel empty, hopeless, and disconnected from others. She may have relationship problems, health problems, or be susceptible to depression, anxiety, or substance abuse. Those dormant painful feelings were not, in fact, swept under the rug after all; they were just insidiously rechannelled into all of the physical and emotional avenues of her life.

One of the most difficult interviews I did for this book was with a man who, by his own admission, skipped the stage of Disorganization. The result is that his life is informed by the deepest despair and sense of utter hopelessness that I encountered. Kevin is a forty-nine-year-old gay man whose identical twin brother, also a gay man, died of AIDS in 1984. Kevin and Larry were extraordinarily close brothers and friends. For the two years and three months of Larry's illness, Kevin was his caretaker. Kevin quit his pursuit of an acting career and devoted himself full-time to Larry's care. It was an all-consuming role.

After Larry's initial diagnosis, Kevin reevaluated his life and realized that he had always wanted a child. So by a series of fortuitous circumstances, he met a lesbian woman who also wanted to raise a child. By the process of artificial insemination, she got pregnant just three weeks before Larry died.

> After Larry's death, Susan was pregnant and I just focused on that. I was so amazed and excited that I was going to have a kid. This thing I really wanted was happening and yet my brother had died. It didn't allow the grief to come. For the next several months, I was planning for the birth of my child, but I was also very, very distraught. Another best friend died of cancer a year later; I didn't even grieve him. I just said, "I can't. I just can't." I couldn't do it.

Kevin jumped into Reconstruction rather than face his feelings of grief. He focused on Susan's pregnancy and eventually on the new baby. He went back to school full time to become a social worker, he sought additional training to become a psychotherapist. He got a full-time job in a hospital working with patients dying of AIDS. He started a new romantic relationship with a man (who later was diagnosed as HIV positive, a fact that Kevin cannot even discuss).

On the surface it might seem that Kevin transcended. After all, he reinvested in a new love. He reinvested in a career change that helped others. He devoted himself to a new life, to his child. But as you listen to Kevin, you hear that he has, in fact, not transcended, and that this is largely due to the fact that he skipped Disorganization. Trying to go from Shock to Reconstruction without first going through—or *eventually* going through—Disorganization is like trying to go from kindergarten to college without first going through all the intervening years of schooling. It just doesn't work. Kevin continued,

There were a lot of obstacles to grieving for me. I've cut off. I've had patients who died. I just cut off the grieving. I don't grieve when people die, at all, I just put it away. I couldn't do this work if I let the grief in. People say, "I don't know how you're functioning because you're doing so much." I imagine that this is all a defense. I'm filling my life up—with all good things, there isn't one bad thing—but it doesn't give me time to think.

The loss of my brother was so cataclysmic to me, I felt like I had died. I had no idea how to be in the world without my brother. I was never an individual—I was always part of a unit. It felt like my entire history disappeared and I had to sort of learn from scratch who I was and what I was doing in the world and how to live in the world. That's how it felt. In order to function, I had to sort of put away the grief. A mechanism kicked in and I just shut it off.

How has cutting off the grief affected him physically, emotionally, spiritually? How does this repressed grief ultimately gnaw at him on a daily basis? The impact of thwarted grief is quite insidious, and powerful.

I think it's really affecting me very badly. I think it's inside—I can feel it. I cry over little things. I start to get an inkling of what I feel in terms of my grief, but as soon as I get an inkling of how the despair is so deep, I just put a lid on it. I think I have to control it because the despair is so great.

I'm also very impatient and very angry, though I don't show it. I project an easygoing, patient person, but I'm angry at little things: waiting in line for something, in the subway. I'm very, very angry. I'm angry that I'm so busy that I don't have a moment to breathe. I'm angry that thirteen years of my life has been devastated by AIDS and it doesn't stop. I'm angry that I'm trapped in this ongoing nightmare that now is a way of life. I just keep the anger inside, so I'm impatient and irritable, things I didn't used to be.

Kevin is now in an intensive psychoanalytic training program (as well as working full-time in the hospital). Part of the requirement for training is being in his own psychoanalysis. I asked if his grief is something he ever addresses in his therapy.

I try to work on it in therapy; I feel like I need to work on it, but I'm very afraid. I'm afraid of what I'll find. I don't have hope at all. I've lost hope totally. I used to be very hopeful and now I just don't have it. The future I have a sense of is horrible; I don't think of it as anything positive at all. It's like nothing really matters, I mean *really* matters. What's the difference? We're all going to die. I don't really have the kind of hope that is carefree, a sense of anticipation, looking forward to things.

Kevin doesn't believe in God, nor does he believe in Larry's eternal spirit or that he'll be reunited with Larry when he dies. He doesn't feel compassionately toward others who have had losses since they can never identify with what it is to lose an identical twin brother. Kevin isn't grateful for the relationship he had and says, "I feel like I wish I never had it, because the pain is so deep that if I hadn't had it then the loss wouldn't be." And Kevin isn't comforted by memories. They are only bitter rather than sweet. He said, "When people talk about Larry, I hate it. It's like, 'How could you talk about him so lightly?' For me, when his name is mentioned it's like a knife in my heart."

I asked Kevin if he thought he could ever revisit the grief and get in touch with some of the pain to free up his emotional blocks. He said,

> Would it be worth it to go into the abyss? I don't know if I ever will. When Larry was in the world, I was anchored on the ground. Now I never touch the ground. I never feel settled or grounded. I feel like it's stone inside. The stone is my grief, this pit of despair. I have created this image that he's just away so I don't have to deal with it. But it's also exhausting. I'm always exhausted. I suspect that it might not be possible to grieve sufficiently where you feel whole again, where you feel okay. I might not feel grounded anyway if I did go into the abyss. It's a weird kind of feeling.

If you grieve sufficiently, do you ever feel whole again? Kevin is right to a degree because a piece of you will always be missing, a piece of you died right when your loved one died. But is it possible to have a meaningful life again, to believe in God, to reach out to other grievers, to have hope and a sense of a positive future, to be comforted by memories, to integrate the loss into your life? The answer is a resounding *yes*. It is possible to transcend the loss. Kevin just shows us that it isn't possible unless you first go into the abyss.

I believe that if Kevin were to face the abyss and to feel the despair, that gradually, over time, he would heal and would therefore feel less hopeless. I think he might not feel compelled to run as much. I think he might even have moments of true inner peace and happiness again. But the only way out is through; that's the bottom line.

Disorganization Revisited

I can't stress enough that *it's never too late* to go back to Disorganization, to take care of unfinished business—no matter how many years have gone by. I hear stories all the time of people who many, many years later go back to grieve. I knew a man who was seventeen years old when his father died. At the time, he wasn't able to fully mourn. When he turned forty-five, however, the age his father was when *he* died, grief came rushing in. This man found himself in therapy finally mourning the death of his father, which had occurred, at that point, twenty-eight years previously.

Similarly, I once had a woman in a grief group who was mourning the death of her fiancé some twenty-two years previously. She called me, tentatively asking if she was eligible to be in a bereavement group, since the loss was from so many years ago. I told her absolutely, that it's never too late to grieve. In the group, she began to grapple with emotional issues that had been buried for nearly a quarter century. She was moved to contact her near in-laws, whom she hadn't spoken to in twenty years, and was able to get some answers to questions never asked. She had a healing experience and reported finally having a sense of inner peace about this issue.

Dr. Harville Hendrix is a prominent couples therapist

who has written extensively on relationship issues and conducts national workshops for couples and professionals. In his highly popular book, *Getting the Love You Want: A Guide for Couples*, Dr. Hendrix discusses his own experience with repressed grief and how he eventually was forced to go back into the abyss. By the time he was six years old, Hendrix had lost both of his parents, but didn't feel much emotional pain. He didn't even cry. He remembers being praised by an older sibling for being such a "brave boy" and took this to mean "you are valued when you are not in touch with your pain."

Hendrix credits his repressed emotions for destroying his first marriage since he was "cut off from an essential part of my being. I was not fully alive." He was not able to be supportive to his wife after her father died as he wondered to himself, "What's the big deal? I lost both of my parents and had felt no pain. Why was she being so emotional?"

It wasn't until later, at the age of thirty-three, that he discovered that he had to go back to the grief, and all the pain and anger and confusion that it entailed. In his training as a psychoanalyst, he was required to be in his own therapy. It was at that time, twenty-seven years after his parents' deaths, that his grief finally opened.

In one of my first sessions, the therapist asked me to tell him about my parents. I told him that they had both died when I was young, but that a lot of good luck had come my way as a result. Because my parents died, I got to live with my sister, get out of south Georgia, get a good education, and so on and so on.

"Tell me about your mother's death," he said to me, cutting short my edited autobiography.

I started to tell him how she died, but for some strange reason my throat felt dry and constricted.

"Tell me about her funeral," he said.

Once again I tried to talk. Then, to my great surprise, I burst into tears. I cried and cried. There was no stopping me. I was thirty-three years old, and I was crying like a six-year-old boy. After a few minutes, my therapist looked at me kindly and said, "Harville, you are just beginning to grieve over your mother's death."

Once I began to experience my own pain and the inevitable rage that accompanied it, I began to change. I was less anxious. I had more compassion for other people's pain. And, for the first time in my conscious memory, I felt fully alive. I know who I was and where I had been, and I felt in tune with the beating of my own heart. All of my senses opened up, and I began to make peace with the world.

Once Hendrix experienced his grief, then he was healed; he was freed up emotionally and he was able to move on to a place of emotional reconstruction.

That's not to say that going back into Disorganization will be easy. You had good reasons for wanting to avoid it in the first place. It takes a lot of courage, support, and trust to go back into the valley of the shadow, particularly when you were hoping you were done. But the only way to journey on to Transcendence, the only way to completely heal, is to fully experience the grief. That's when true healing will begin, and it's never too late to initiate that process.

Stuck in Disorganization

What if one experiences the grief, but never moves on? What if one remains immersed in the feelings of anger, sadness, anxiety, and despair? The second major type of grief dysfunction is getting stuck in Disorganization. You see, some grievers are so successful with the stage of Disorganization—experiencing and expressing the feelings—that they never stop. One griever I spoke with said, "I've seen so many people hold onto grief. My grandmother's been holding onto grief for forty-five years. She hasn't been able to move on." She hasn't denied, avoided, or delayed her grief, she's holding onto it for dear life.

The chronic mourner, or the perpetually bereaved, puts life on hold and invests his identity solely in being a griever, thus arresting growth in any new direction. Dr. Forrest Church, senior minister at the Unitarian Church of All Souls in New York City, and author of *LIFE LINES: Holding On (and Letting Go)*, points out that, "Once the death of another person becomes an excuse for not going on with one's own life, or not being able to live fully and abundantly, then that's pathological."

While for some people, being stuck in Disorganization is obvious—they effectively stop living—for many others, being stuck in Disorganization is more subtle, more insidious. The griever may appear to have gone on with life—to continue to work and function—but they haven't really reconstructed *emotionally*. Their emotional life and their emotional growth may be crippled to the extent that they have trouble having or maintaining interpersonal relationships. Generally with this type of scenario, the functioning griever has gotten blocked by a particular feeling that inhibits their full emotional growth and development.

BLOCKED BY PAIN

Ironically, for many people, pain is a sort of comfort because it is a link to the deceased. The pain equals connection. Therefore, the unspoken assumption is that if you give up the pain, you'll somehow give up the loved one. Furthermore, the concept of "moving on" brings up feelings of guilt because not only will you be in danger of "forgetting" your loved one if you move on with life, but also you feel disloyal to be happy again when your loved one is dead.

Myrtle is a sixty-two-year-old widow who is still deeply pained by the death of her husband, which occurred nearly eight years ago. She told me, "There isn't a day that I don't think of him. We were only married for four years, but they were the happiest years of my life. A part of me left when he left—I don't feel like a whole person anymore. It's depressing to talk about." As she told me this, she began crying so hard that she had to excuse herself from the interview to compose herself.

The pain for Myrtle, even eight years later, is overpowering. Although she's lonely, she could never consider being involved with another man again. She said, "I cannot let go of Douglas completely. I'll never let go completely. And I could never get mixed up with anybody else because I don't ever want to replace him."

She cannot, in many ways, accept that he is gone. "I still cannot understand why he, a good man, was taken, when there are so many others who don't care whether they live or die." She still has difficulty sleeping at night, and often finds it hard to be in their apartment. She would never consider moving, however, for that would be a betrayal. She told me that it's hardest to be in their apartment on special holidays or anniversaries.

Myrtle is comforted by her belief that Douglas is waiting for her in heaven, and actually looks forward to dying. She's hoping that once they're reunited, she'll finally feel whole again. Myrtle works hard to keep the pain at bay, but she told me that she's basically just killing time until she dies.

Myrtle, in many ways, is stuck in Disorganization because she is blocked by her pain. It keeps her connected to Douglas, but it also keeps her from moving on and from growing emotionally.

BLOCKED BY IDEALIZATION

Idealizing your loved one is a type of blockage that often prevents forward growth. No one is perfect, and no relationship is perfect either. If a mourner can recognize this fact, accepting all aspects of the person who died—the pros and cons, assets and faults—then they generally have an easier time moving through the stages of grief. However, if the relationship with the deceased was fraught with either overt or covert conflict and ambivalence while the loved one was alive, sometimes grief gets skewed into a false idealization. In other words, if you cannot acknowledge or tolerate that conflict, then you unconsciously flip the ambivalence to adoration, thereby assuaging your guilt. Unfortunately the result is often stunted emotional growth.

Mary is a thirty-four-year-old woman whose father died in 1979 when she was sixteen years old. He hadn't been ill. He had no history of health problems. But one day, Mary came home after school and saw a police car in front of her house. She saw a neighbor outside and she asked, "What happened?" When the neighbor told her that Mary's father had passed away from a massive heart attack, Mary's knees buckled, she fainted, and life has never been the same.

Mary generally dates men old enough to be her father, and she clearly had a terrible time speaking with me about her father's death. She couldn't maintain eye contact with me when she discussed her father and seemed highly anxious throughout our interview. Mary is having trouble reconstructing her emotional life and moving on with her grief. One of the tip-offs to me was when she said, "My mother is really angry at my dad, but I don't like to hear her anger. I can't hear her talking about her resentments. I'm very sensitive to criticism about my father. Yeah, I know I idealize him. I know he screwed up my brothers, but I don't want to talk about his bad qualities."

However, she told me earlier that he never paid much attention to her, that he often ignored her, he had an explosive temper, he yelled at the kids for being too noisy, and he was overly concerned with pushing them all to succeed. But after losing her father, she says that she can't get over feeling cheated, that this devastating loss sums her up, that there's a missing piece to her life.

Because Mary cannot accept her father's imperfections, she unconsciously is seeking to duplicate the lost perfect relationship with the perfect older man, hence her choice to date much older men. However, she seeks to replicate a relationship that not only cannot exist now, but never existed in the past either.

Mary is in therapy now and hopefully that process will help her to unravel the internal emotional tangle that is ultimately affecting her quality of life and her ability to be in a committed romantic relationship. Part of that process is integrating the whole of who your deceased loved one was— all that you loved about him or her, including the good, the not so good, and the human imperfections.

BLOCKED BY ANGER

If years after your loss you are still holding onto anger with a vengeance, it is a signal that energy has gotten stuck in Disorganization. Whenever a huge piece of your energy has gotten locked onto something from the past, it implies that a sense of moving on has been thwarted. Again, trying to view the situation from a realistic, multifaceted point of view is what leads to healing.

Harry is a fifty-year-old man who realized that something was wrong when three years after his brother's death, he was still mired in anger. He said, "I thought it was about his dying, then I realized that I wasn't angry about his dying, I was having trouble with the relationship we had while he was alive." So Harry knew that there was emotional work to be done.

A friend of mine said to me, "Can't you think of anything positive about Steve? I thought he was a nice guy." So he suggested that I sit down and write a letter and list only positive things about him. So I sat down and wrote a letter. Believe me, it took awhile. But something changed inside. I finally decided that I was going to see things in a different way, that I was going to turn it around.

It's not easy, but you can change your relationship with somebody after they're dead. It would have been better if I had done it while he was alive, but the key to my grieving was realizing this. And that's when I started the real mourning process—then it was easy.

Trying to see all that a person is may not be an easy process. Letting go of extreme emotions is always difficult. But unless you do it, you might be blocked in your ability to move on with life. And once you do it, the rest may not exactly be easy, but the process will flow more readily.

Maureen is a thirty-five-year-old woman who had every reason to hate her father. He sexually abused her from the time she was four until she was thirteen. In 1989 he was diagnosed with lung cancer. Maureen said, "His illness was especially hard for me. How do you deal with your sick, dying, pathetic father when all you feel for him is rage and disgust and fear?" Maureen never made peace with him. In fact, until the day he died, he never admitted to the incest.

When he died shortly after his diagnosis, Maureen shut down. She didn't grieve; she felt happy that he was dead. But when her life wasn't working out the way she wanted, she started therapy. She started to grieve, and as time went by, she realized that she was stuck in all of her many conflicted feelings.

In the last two years [fourteen years after his death], I've grieved a lot for my father, and I've been angry at him for all the unresolved things. There's still so much unexpressed anger that I haven't even gotten to yet. I don't feel like I've finished grieving yet. I need to get through more of the emotional stuff about the incest. It's so blocked up. All the hard feelings, I'm afraid to feel. But those hard feelings are the gateway to the soft feelings—grief and love.

I have this goal to learn to accept my father so I can love him again. Part of me thinks he's a villain but he did the best he could. He was messed up but he tried his best; that's a new thing for me to say. He gave it his best and it wasn't very good, but it was the best he could do. [He was also sexually abused as a child and from a family of alcoholics.]

Maureen may have more grief work to attend to, but she has already grown substantially. Part of her healing was the need to see *both* sides of her father, the good and the bad.

I just know that wherever I'm going to go in my life and in my future relationships is going to depend a lot on my resolving what I feel about my father. I allow myself to think about him a lot, which is nice, because I didn't used to. It's hard for me to think about the good things; it's hard for me to admit there could be good things and the bad things. For a long time I made him all bad, in contrast to when I was a child and he was all good. Now I want to find a balance.

Maureen said that the process she's embarked upon is already freeing her emotionally as well as spiritually. She had previously rejected religion since her father had been a practicing Catholic. But working through her grief and her conflicted feelings has helped her to rediscover her spiritual center.

It delights me that I'm still capable of being spiritual. I've been a little flower that was shriveled up, and now there's sunshine up there. It was a direct result from dealing with the grief. When I had to come to terms with the death of my parent and come to terms with all the bad stuff, I ended up taking a lot more responsibility for my life. Not for what he did to me, but for my life now. How long can I go on blaming my dead father for why I'm not where I want to be and why I'm not the person I want to be? Yeah, he's to blame for what he did, but you know, I'm thirty-five and that stuff happened a long time ago and I've been doing a lot of work to get past it. His death allows me to stop focusing on him and to put more focus on me and what I'm going to do to get beyond it. I don't want to be holding onto this my whole life, I want to get past it.

Maureen is on a journey of revisiting Disorganization, getting unstuck, coming to terms with all that her father was—both bad and good—and consequently she's moving on with her life in Reconstruction and even having glimmers of Transcendence.

BLOCKED BY GUILT

Many people find that they cannot move on emotionally because they feel so guilty, guilty about the death, guilty about the life. There's always something that we wish we had said or done. Bereaved parents inevitably feel responsible and believe that they should have or could have prevented their child's death. Or people punish themselves because they didn't do all of the perfect things that in hindsight they wish they had done. The potential list for guilt offenses is endless.

Remember Barbara, our SOAR traveler? She had to wrestle with the issue of guilt. After all, she had effectively turned her back on her brother Bobby because of his lifestyle and his homosexuality. She had drifted from him, judged him. There were many years of estrangement that she could never get back. Her grief could have left her trapped in the "if onlys."

The trouble with death is that you can't say you're sorry. The great sadness is that it's too late. Death is the ultimate too late. You absolutely can't catch up. So, after a while, the terrible, terrible remorse sinks in. I remember that I was at church on Good Friday and the minister was talking about remorse, and the biblical passage was about Peter who, if anybody would have remorse it was Peter, who denied that he knew Jesus. Jesus had told him that he would deny Him and Peter said, no, no, he never would. But of course he does, and Jesus turns around and says, "This is the rock on which I will build my church." I heard it, I really heard that for the first time. I thought what an extraordinary act that this person has denied your existence and yet, you turn and you embrace him.

What came to mind as I was listening to this, what I realized, was if you live in remorse, you live backwards. You aren't moving ahead in any way; you are living in the past. All my Buddhist studies had emphasized the importance of being present, present now. I couldn't force the remorse away; but that day, with that realization, that that was living backwards, it just lifted.

When you get stuck in Disorganization for whatever reason—by pain, idealization, anger, guilt—when you fail to move on to Reconstruction, you are living backwards. And the point of healing from grief is to be living forwards.

Working through the Complications

I'd like to look at one woman's experience of coming back from the brink of complicated mourning and how her journey eventually took her onto several pathways toward Transcendence. Hope is a thirty-three-year-old author and a motherless daughter. I discussed her story in chapter 7 in the context of Outreach, but I think it's interesting to note that she didn't get to Transcendence without a lot of difficult, complicated grief work.

Hope's mother was diagnosed with breast cancer when Hope was fifteen years old. Neither Hope nor her mother expected that the cancer would be terminal. Hope was seventeen when she did find out that her mother was dying, just a few days before she actually died. Hope said,

After she died, there was a sense in my family that this is not the time to be angry; this is not the time to be upset; this is the time to concentrate on surviving. We're going to figure out how we're going to get from day to day without Mom here. That needs to be our focus in the immediate future. It became a matter of habit, perhaps, the way we coped over the long term— at least for the next seven years in my case—to not talk about the loss, to not talk about how we felt about it, either the details or the emotions.

My memories of those years are fuzzy. I think I expended so much energy pretending that it wasn't a dramatic event and that it didn't affect me profoundly. I have a lot of white space in my memory. It was very difficult when I was writing my book to go back and revisit some of those months; I think I suppressed a lot. I completely blocked out the hospital scenes during the last few days before my mother's death until I was probably twenty-three or twenty-four. I remember it slowly coming back to me in pieces when I was ready to focus on it. That was with the help of a very compassionate friend, and I also started seeing a therapist at that time.

What were those seven years of repressed grief like for Hope?

During those seven years, I was very determined to be independent and self-sufficient. The way I chose to do that was by becoming very, very career focused. I was very intent on getting good grades in college, on procuring internships, on doing extracurricular activities that would advance me in journalism. That was my means of insuring that I wouldn't have to depend on my family. I think it was little more than a survival method.

Also, there were periodic and unpredictable displays of vulnerability that left me quite shaken, because I at seventeen, eighteen, nineteen was trying so hard to convince myself that I was invulnerable. In terms of emotional vulnerability, I think I was trying to convince myself that I was an emotional fortress. Every now and then a life event would occur that would clearly show me that the opposite was true. That would shake me up quite a lot, because I wasn't willing or ready to admit that there was any vulnerability.

When unpredictable things happened to me, I'd go ballistic. I'd have temper tantrums.

What was it that finally led Hope back into Disorganization seven years after her mother's death? She said there probably was a "slow evolution toward that awareness over the seven years as I moved further and further from my mother's death and realized that it wasn't getting any easier for me to cope with it, especially as I started going through life transitions that were very painful to encounter or experience without her there, like graduating from college, starting my first job."

Then Hope had a trigger loss, a loss that was mildly traumatic in and of itself, but that triggered all of the unresolved grief for her mother that lay beneath the surface. She broke off an engagement with the man she expected to marry. Although it was her choice, the loss sent her reeling.

There were moments when I thought I wouldn't live through it, because I was losing not just him, but I was also losing that parent figure again. It was really the breakup of the engagement, I think, that sent me to do the intense grief work for my mother because I realized that though I missed him terribly, I was mourning the loss of a protector and an emotional caretaker in my life. It sent me right back to do the mother-loss work.

It was a terrifying emotional crisis—a moment when she literally froze in time in the middle of the street—that made her realize she had a great deal of emotional work to do and that she needed help to do it.

The event in the middle of the street was oddly metaphoric. I was trying to get from one place to another, and I was trapped in one place. I became rooted to the spot in the middle of the street. I was very close to some kind of psychological edge, and I don't think I ever went over it, but I got close. I just stood there in the street for one minute, two minutes—I don't even know how long it was. Time expands and contracts in bizarre ways when you're having an emotional crisis. Ultimately I did get to the distant side of the street, not where I began but where I was headed for, and at that point I realized I needed more help than good friends or coworkers could offer me. It's possible that the feelings of vulnerability had reached a crescendo to an extent where I couldn't pretend I didn't miss my mother anymore.

So Hope began to grieve. She went back into Disorganization. She went into counseling and said that by "talking about it and talking about it and talking about it, I started opening up the sealed box, very slowly so the memories came back in bits and pieces." Just previous to starting therapy, Hope spent five days in an intensive therapy program that had an emphasis on psychodrama. She credits this too for helping her to do her grief work.

There was empty chair work, there was pounding the pillows, there were all of those techniques that are considered useful in dealing with an adult who had a disruptive or difficult childhood and has quite a lot of anger and resentment as a result. I was very surprised and a little shaken by the depth of my anger. When we were doing individual psychodramatic work, I started off speaking to my mother very calmly. Within the span of ten to fifteen minutes, I was crying uncontrollably and shouting at her, "How could you have left us?"

I didn't know that that sense of abandonment was in me because I'd spent so much time either focused on other things or trying to avoid it. I expended an enormous amount of energy on avoidance, and I realized how tightly wound I had been for all of those years. There always existed the threat that I would cross the line into that emotional territory, and I couldn't risk that because I didn't feel there was anyone who would be able to help me through. Finally I felt that I had a safe place to feel those emotions. I walked out of there feeling as if a weight had been lifted off of my shoulders. That's what helped me do it, but there was a delay of seven years before I got there.

Hope points out that this work doesn't have to be faced alone and that often the supportive presence of a person or people is exactly what is needed in order to plunge into the abyss.

Doing the grief work opened Hope to a less rigid, more flexible way of living. It freed her emotionally from the traps of fear and control. She said, "Doing the grief work allowed me to see shades of gray in my life, and to welcome them and to welcome change in a way that I was not able to do between the ages of seventeen and twenty-four because I did not allow for any possibility for change or for any unpredictability in my life."

When Hope finally went through Disorganization—seven years after her mother's death—she didn't get stuck in any of the feelings of pain, anger, or guilt because she flowed with the process rather than resisting it. She also maintained a healthy, balanced relationship with her mother by recalling the bad ("We had a very, very feisty, very difficult relationship for most of my adolescence") as well as the good ("My mother was a very charitable and selfless person").

By experiencing Disorganization, Hope was able to move on to Reconstruction. And ultimately she found a *channel* for her grief, which swept her onward toward Transcendence. She began researching and writing the book *Motherless Daughters*. The idea was sparked for her before graduate school but gained momentum there when a professor encouraged her efforts. After graduate school she began to seriously pursue it and started interviewing women to find out if they felt the same way she did after losing their mothers.

I think I began with the interviews because I was seeking to normalize my own experience, to get a sense that what I was feeling would be characterized as normal long-term grief. The women I met with were clearly still mourning the loss of their mothers even though they had gone on in every other respect, or most other respects, to have very happy and productive and fulfilling lives. That was a source of great encouragement to me. I found that practically all the women were telling me the same story, which was that they still missed their mothers, in some cases twenty-five or thirty years after she had died.

Hope said that writing the book "helped me integrate my mother's death into my life in a way that felt comfortable rather than very sad or very frightening." And as you know, the book touched a nerve among women internationally, making it a best-seller and spawning the nationwide organization Motherless Daughters.

In doing her grief work, in researching and writing the book, and in working with other motherless daughters, Hope was able to get back on track with her grief. Getting through complicated grief, just like getting through complicated spirituality, involves active, external work mixed with a conscious and conscientious internal quest.

My very strong feeling is that having put so much time and work into this subject matter, and examining the loss of my mother and its effect on me, I really do feel that I'm "caught up" in my mourning. I don't feel that I suffer from arrested development to the degree that I might have five or six years ago. I feel my age. I don't feel that a big piece of me is stuck back at seventeen anymore. I feel that I've mourned to the best of my capacity at the age of thirty-one, that I've caught up, that I did the mourning that I hadn't done during those intervening seven years, and that now I'm where I should be in the mourning process.

But that doesn't by any means mean that I think I'm done. I know that there will be transitional events that I hit that will make me grieve for my mother all over again. I know that those will be childbirth if I have a child; it will be reaching her age at the time of death, which was only forty-two, among other things.

Hope reminds us that even as you finish the grief work (the acute grief in Disorganization), the grieving process in general is never "over" because you are forever affected by your loss.

Moving On to Synthesis

You *will* be affected by this loss forever. But that is different from being stuck in the various feelings of Disorganization; it is different from having emotional blocks that prevent you from fully enjoying life and love. I hope I've convinced you that it's possible to regrieve at any time; it's possible to get "caught up" with your mourning. But you will still have to face Synthesis, which is a key to the gateway of Transcendence. Just as it is never too late to grieve, it is never too late to embrace Synthesis, to make the loss meaningful, and thereby to transcend. Our last chapter will take a final look at this possibility and this opportunity.

PART V

Getting Back on Track

CHAPTER 12

It's Never Too Late to Transcend

The main thing is that you hear life's music everywhere. Most people hear only its dissonances.
—THEODOR FONTANE

There is an old apple tree in New Hampshire that produces more fruit than any other apple tree in the area. When you see it during the fruit-bearing season, it is heavily laden, overflowing with the sweetest, most delicious apples you've ever tasted. Why is this particular tree so bountiful? Local residents will tell you to go look at the trunk of the tree. Upon inspection, you will see that the trunk is severely scarred, as it has been struck by lightning, hacked, cut, and burnt at various times in its long history. And yet, despite it all, this tree has lived with its losses through the years and has actually been strengthened and fortified by its tragedies. The richest-producing fruit tree in New Hampshire is an example of Transcendence!

Living with loss through the years, for some people,

means going on to live a life full of meaning and joy, a life of fruitful abundance. They are the ones who have transcended. But as you know, living with loss through the years for other people means living an embittered, frozen existence. They are the ones who have gotten stuck somewhere and require intervention to help them move on. Ultimately, living with loss through the years is as individual as the very individuals who grieve.

But one important element for healthy adaptation to loss, and certainly a vital key in unlocking the door to Transcendence, is Synthesis. Before grievers can peacefully live with the loss, and before they can transcend, they need to understand, accept, and embrace Synthesis into their lives. It is the hinge upon which rests a healthy future.

About Synthesis

Synthesis, as we've discussed, refers to the retriggered feelings, the ongoing dialogue, connection, and memories of your loved one that are important strands woven into the fabric of your life. Like the sober alcoholic who recovers but is never recovered, the griever heals but is never healed. You can reconstruct your life and you can even reach Transcendence, but you cannot erase the loss from your life.

Don and Florence, who lost their twenty-two-year-old son fifteen years ago, sum up the ongoing nature of Synthesis. Florence said, "We've accepted that he's dead but we still grieve. We feel that the grief that goes on is a grief that can continue to be healthy." Don added, "I cannot deny that I miss him, and I don't want to not miss him. We can't forget him. The hard part of it will never go away but neither will the wonderful part of his life and who he was ever go away."

One of the most heart-wrenching stories that I heard while researching this book was of a woman who suffered the most unimaginable tragedy: both of her young sons died within nine months of each other. That was forty-four years ago when Regina was thirty years old. First, her youngest child, Brad, who was almost three at the time, died of leukemia. Shortly after, Jerry, who was five, was also diagnosed with leukemia and died within a few weeks.

Imagine the excruciating pain with two such immense losses. Imagine the sense of injustice. She did eventually work through the grief. She was able to get in touch with her anger—anger at God for letting her children suffer, anger at God for taking her children away, and even anger toward her children "for leaving and abandoning me—I know it seems so irrational, but I did."

As the years passed, Regina went on to graduate school, to live life. She had two more healthy children, who are now adults, she now has several grandchildren, and she became active in a church community. Now it has been nearly half a century since those deaths, but do you think she's "over them"? Do you think she ever still feels the sadness and the sorrow of those early losses? She told me, "As time goes on, what you lose is the memory of the suffering first. That kind of fades to a degree. But it's never not sad. I still hate to see those children denied life." And does she still think of them? Are they a continuing part of her life even after so many years? She affirms, "I still think about them. They're part of you in some basic way. There's still a sense of frustration because they should survive you and they didn't." The impact of loss lasts a lifetime.

Resisting Synthesis

As we have seen, avoidance and resistance are in some ways even more treacherous and more painful than grief itself. Resisting Synthesis, avoiding the process of integrating life with loss, eventually causes myriad life difficulties.

Ronald lost his eleven-year-old son Jason just over thirteen years ago. In some important ways, Ron has done his grief work and moved on. But in other profound ways, Ron cannot accept his son's death and, in particular, he cannot accept its ongoing impact in his life.

Jason was an accomplished singer and pianist, like his father, who is a professional musician. Ron said, "He was a very sensitive child, way beyond his years. He was very peaceful and very wise, and he was my best friend." Ron was a very active father, spending lots of time with both his son and his daughter. He said, "My children were always so mature. We went to shows, concerts; I read to them all the time. They never gave me a hard time. We had fun together all the time. Being with them was my main joy in life."

But one day, Jason was killed in a freak accident. He was on the beach with friends when a kite blew onto the section of the beach where they played. Jason and his friends chased the kite and Jason touched it at the exact moment when a piece of its copper wiring touched six inches of exposed power line. Jason was killed instantly.

Ron was absolutely devastated. He was touring in Europe at the time and found out over the phone. He remembers screaming into the receiver, "You mean I'll never see him again?" Initially nothing helped to ease the pain. But he did what he needed to do in the stage of Disorganization. He talked, he cried.

> I was talking to people constantly. That was the only thing on my mind. I dumped it on everybody. I told everyone, whether it was appropriate or not—people in grocery lines. I couldn't even stand up straight, I was crying all the time. I was literally bent over. I cried for like a year and a half every day, until one day, I woke up a little bit happy. I knew that the crisis was over. I heard birds singing. I knew that the grieving was moving to a different level, a better, healthier level. I saw a glimmer and I knew that Jason would want me to be happy. There's a part of you that will always feel the pain, but there's another part of you that should go on.

Ron believes in a spiritual realm. He believes in God though he doesn't practice in an organized religion. He believes in reincarnation. Ron has an attitude of gratitude when he says, "I was blessed having him for eleven years. How else can I look at it? I had this angel for eleven years and I have another angel now [his surviving daughter]. Bach lost eleven children. He had twenty-one children and half of them died in early childhood. How did he cope? Look at the music he wrote."

Ron believes that Jason's soul lives on. That belief brings Ron comfort and peace. "If I didn't have that belief, I don't know how I would have survived. I would have dwelled on his suffering. But my belief is that he was immediately released from bondage and went to a better place. It has sustained me from the very beginning."

He believes that Jason's death was part of a plan. He says, "I know we have free choice, but I think our basic fate is sealed. His mission was to be here for eleven years, that's it. It was his time, for whatever reason. He gathered the knowledge he needed to move on and to come back as a higher being. It helps for me to accept it." Ron is comforted by his belief system and says, "I guess I consider myself lucky to believe in all this."

On the surface, it sounds like Ron accepts Synthesis. It even sounds like Ron transcended in some ways. When I interviewed him I found his courage admirable and the depth of his pain palpable. And yet something is not quite right for Ron. Ron is still tormented by his loss.

To begin with, he has never visited the cemetery in all these thirteen years.

> I haven't been to the cemetery. I'm afraid. I'll have to face it . . . standing right in front of him, driving there. It's just so intense. Everybody tells me you have to go to the cemetery, you should go to the cemetery, it will be a release. I don't do it, maybe I should. Maybe it will be good for me. I do want to and I don't. Why should I go and look at a grave? Why should I have to see where my little boy is buried? I don't want to see it. It's like rubbing my nose in it.

Ron never observes important anniversary days, such as the death day, because it brings up too much pain. He doesn't want to be reminded of Jason's death.

> Once my wife was lighting candles for Jason. She was hesitant to tell me what it was for. I said, "Don't

do that ever again. Don't remind me; I don't want to be reminded." I can't watch television or movies that have the death of a child in it. Forget it. Even my mom doesn't remind me of the date of the event. I don't recognize the death day. It's not a tough day if I'm not reminded of it. There's always some pain. Who wants pain?

Ron says that he is insulted if somebody has the nerve to mention Jason's name. He finds it painful, intrusive.

I would never remind somebody of their loss. I hate when people do it to me. Even my wife has to be careful. She knows she has to be careful. She just mentions the word Jason and I jump; I'm shocked. She used to do that, she didn't know any better.

Contrast this position with the transcendent attitude of Beverly, whose daughter died of AIDS, who said, "It's a present when somebody remembers her name. They just mention her name and it's like somebody giving me the most wonderful, biggest gift."

Yet try as he might to suppress any ongoing feelings and associations with Jason, clearly Ron is still affected. His unconscious betrays the depth of his ongoing struggle when he tells me that he has regular "tortured dreams" about Jason.

I never go more than a few months without dreaming about him. It's a mixture of pleasure and pain. I wake up smiling and sometimes it's nice to be visited. But it still hurts. It's never long enough and it's never just joyful. Something puts a damper on it because I know he's only visiting from heaven for a very short time.

Ron knows that the pain is there; he knows that Synthesis is a reality. But he seems to be conflicted about this reality.

The pain is not good to have. It works on different levels. I think I carry around unhealthy pain, deep down, about it. I would like my belief—my knowledge that he is in a better place, that he's happy, and I was blessed having him—why can't that be the principal, the benefit? Why can't it benefit me? Obviously I'm still burdened by the loss, the grief. In my heart I say, "All right, fine, but why did he have to be taken from me?" I didn't even have a chance to say goodbye. It's just that it seems so incredibly unfair.

Somebody told me, "It never goes away." That sticks with you. On the one hand, it dogs you, that statement, like self-fulfilling prophecy. On the other hand, it's just sort of an affirmation, a good affirmation that I'm allowed to feel grief. There will always be a piece of me that's sad.

I'm not reminded of my pain all the time, even though I have it. I guess it's obvious that I do, even though I don't talk about it. It's still there, sapping my energy. Maybe there's something that's eating away at me, something negative which has prevented me from being whole again.

Certainly there could be other reasons why Ron is still in so much pain, but I think part of the reason is that Ron resists Synthesis. And yet, I also believe that Ron is working to change this, that he's ultimately on the path to accepting Synthesis. First of all, he consciously knows that the effects of his loss are forever; he believes in Synthesis. Secondly, he started performing "death-related" music, such as requiems, again. He said, "The loss affected my music. Music that dealt with death, I couldn't do it anymore. I still have a hard time doing it. I'm only coming around to doing it now. I did one two years ago. I barely got through it, but I did it. I felt I had to try again."

And finally, Ron consented to doing this interview. He, more than anyone else, was afraid of the interview, of what it would stir up. He asked me repeatedly beforehand if it would be too painful, afraid that the feelings would overwhelm him. But he conquered his fears and faced it. He agreed to the interview, which lasted more than two hours. Unlike another bereaved parent who refused to let me interview her because, she said, "Oh, I'm over that. It's not an issue in my life anymore," Ron knows that it is an issue, forever. And it's never too late to accept Synthesis.

Moving On to Transcendence

Synthesis is the gateway to Transcendence, because once you accept that you are forever changed and that life is forever different, you have to ask, "What are you going to do about that fact? Will the change be for better or for worse?" It's the loss itself that becomes the catalyst for meaning. Each of the pathways toward Transcendence is about changes that occurred *because* of the loss. Once you accept Synthesis—that the loss is forever—this acceptance can fuel the positive changes that make up Transcendence. And just as it is never too late to grieve, or to accept Synthesis, it is never too late to make up your mind to transcend.

Janice, in her fifties and the mother of four children, is also a social worker and director of a hospice program. I interviewed her to get another professional opinion on this aspect of death and dying. She told me how important it is, in working in this field, to be undergirded by a faith and a personal philosophy, to have some sense of integrating death as a part of life. She talked about how vital a service it is to validate the dying process and to provide support for the family during the process and after the process.

She should know how important this is, because it's the very type of support that she did not receive some thirty years ago after her first child died unexpectedly in a hospital. It was when I asked her how she got interested in this field that she shared her experience with me. She said,

> We lost our first child. She was a year old. That was in the mid-sixties. Sensitivity, awareness, preparation— all those things—were just so absent at that time. I remember being told of the death of our child in a stair- well of a hospital. We went in to see her, she had died, she was removed. We wanted to know what had hap- pened. She had died of a heart illness. Clearly, she was hospitalized, so we knew that she wasn't doing well, but when we went into the hospital and the bed was empty, and the child was gone. . . . [She softly cries.] The physician literally told us in the stairwell that the baby had died. It was just really that crass.

Janice grieved, disorganized, and reconstructed. She re-
sumed her life. She went on to have four more children, to
raise them, and later to go to graduate school in social work.
Eventually she and her family moved to a new community
and she saw an ad in the newspaper for a hospice social
worker. She decided to inquire. During the interview, as she
discovered more about hospice, she kept thinking to herself,
"This is a really needed and valued service that would be
deeply appreciated. I wish I had had this service nearly
twenty years ago."

Twenty years after her loss, Janice chose reinvestment in
a new career to make her loss meaningful. She said, "I didn't
knowingly seek it out, but my loss eventually led me here,
to this field, and it fuels my conviction and energy and resolution to keep doing the work well and make sure that we
ease and help patients and families as much as we can."
Janice also accepts the powers of Synthesis.

I think the resolution of loss probably takes a lifetime
in different ways. That doesn't mean you're not func-
tional, you're not operational, you're not coping with
life issues, but it's a part of your experience just as any
other life experience would be, and I don't think that
one shelves that or gets over that.

As you listen to Janice, you hear the transcendental qualities.

Hopefully, people use their issues of loss and grief
for their own understanding, for the betterment of the
world in which we live, however you might do that.
Each new loss is a challenge because it triggers old

losses. I feel good about taking that experience, working through some of that anger and hostility and using it in a creative way. I think that everything that comes along to you is an opportunity to learn by or get different insights from. But it took me a long time to learn that.

Life brings all kinds of things to you, both wondrous and troublesome for you to deal with, and to me that's a part of my life experience and that's a part of my challenge, and that's a part of my trust and that's a part of my growth.

SOARing to New Heights

I think you will see from having read this book that there are all types of ways to grieve, all types of ways to reconstruct, and all types of ways to find meaning. Which is no surprise, since each of us is unique and each of our experiences is so individual. And yet, we learn from example. We learn from each other as we model each other's behaviors. My hope is that some of the stories here will give you ideas, will provide inspiration for your journey, and will help you see solutions where before had been only problems.

And I hope that the SOAR model will provide you with a framework in which to explore issues of meaning and transcendence. I hope you will be able to use it as somewhat of a road map to guide you on this powerful and emotional journey through the years.

Remember, each of the pathways is about change and a meaningful response to loss. *Spirituality* is working through spiritual and religious issues of anger and doubt to find a richer, enlarged relationship with the Divine. *Outreach* is giving back to others, turning from victim to healer, touching others' lives and in so doing, touching yourself. *Attitude* is focusing on the good and not only on the bad, on what was gained as well as what was lost. (I received a thank-you card from a widow who had been married to her husband for fifty-six years. He had suffered a cruel and slow demise due to Alzheimer's disease. She wrote in her note that, "I know love always leaves behind more than death takes away." A simple, yet poetic reflection of a transcendent attitude.) And finally, *Reinvestment* is finding a channel for the grief. If grief is a heavy toxic gas, then Reinvestment is channeling this toxic gas out through an exhaust pipe. There it escapes into the air and the human psyche functions smoothly. If you don't find a way to channel it out, the noxious fumes spread throughout the psyche, causing disease and distress.

The Miracle of Life and Death

Hearing the stories of so many grievers and transcenders made working on this book at times painful, but mostly inspiring and hopeful. That people do lose and love, that they do shatter and rebuild, that they do transcend their losses is nothing short of miraculous.

The mystery is not that we die, but that we live at all. Life really is the sweetest, most precious gift. And it surrounds us daily. I find this particularly evident during early spring when nature herself is reborn. Have you ever stopped to look at the small spring buds on a tree about to burst forth after a long and cold winter? Or to look at the sprout from a crocus or hyacinth bulb just pushing its way through the recently thawed earth? Every year spring comes to revive the frozen landscape. And every year it is, in my mind, an ordinary, yet extraordinary miracle.

And the fact that humans can be broken and become stronger at the broken places is also one of the most profound and touching of all miracles. I hope that this book has validated what you know in your heart of hearts to be true, that you are forever changed by this loss, by so many losses. And I hope that this book has also shown you that while grief is a lifelong process, it is a potentially meaningful and transcendent one.

It is possible to turn the bitter lemon into lemonade. There are hundreds of ways to make lemonade; you just need to find your own recipe. The SOAR framework will provide you with some of the critical ingredients. Be patient with yourself. It takes time to find your way, time to heal. But you can definitely take responsibility for your own healing. Just remember to take all the love that was good, all the joy that you shared, all the beauty that your loved one embodied, and even all the pain that wrenches your heart and the confusion that burns in your soul—take all of that and transform it to enrich this world. Let the loss touch you and, in turn, let your response touch the world.

May God bless you on your journey.

SUGGESTED READING

Ascher, Barbara Lazear. *Landscape Without Gravity*. New York: Penguin Books, 1993.

Bloomfield, Harold MD, Melba Colgrove, PhD, and Peter McWilliams. *How to Survive the Loss of a Love*. Los Angeles, CA: Prelude Press. 1991.

Bowlby, John. *Attachment and Loss*. New York: Basic Books, 1969.

Church, Forrest. *LIFE LINES: Holding On (and Letting Go)*. Boston: Beacon Press, 1996.

Cousins, Norman. *Anatomy of an Illness*. New York: Bantam Books, 1979.

Dane, Barbara and Samuel Miller. *AIDS: Intervening with Hidden Grievers*. Westport, Conn.: Auburn House, 1992.

Doka, Kenneth and John D. Morgan (editors). *Death and Spirituality*. Amityville, NY: Baywood Publishers, 1993.

Edelman, Hope. *Motherless Daughters*. New York: Delta Publishing, 1994.

Frankl, Viktor. *Man's Search for Meaning*. New York: Simon & Schuster, 1984.

Grollman, Earl. *Living When a Loved One Has Died*. Boston: Beacon Press, 1995.

James, John and Frank Cherry. *The Grief Recovery Handbook*. New York: Harper & Row, 1988.

Krauss, Pesach and Morrie Goldfischer. *Why Me? Coping with Grief, Loss, and Change*. New York: Bantam Books, 1988.

Kübler-Ross, Elisabeth. *On Death and Dying*. New York: Macmillan Publishing Company, 1969.

Kushner, Harold. *When Bad Things Happen to Good People*. New York: Avon Books, 1981.

Lightner, Candy and Nancy Hathaway. *Giving Sorrow Words*. New York: Warner Books, 1990.

Lord, Janice Harris. *No Time for Goodbyes*. Ventura, Calif.: Pathfinder Publishing of California, 1995.

Miller, James. *What Will Help Me?* Fort Wayne, Ind.: Willowgreen Pub, 1994.

Murry, William. *A Faith for All Seasons: Liberal Religion and the Crises of Life*. Bethesda, Md.: River Road Press, 1990.

Rando, Therese. *How to Go On Living When Someone You Love Dies*. New York: Bantam Books, 1991.

Rosen, Elliot J. *Families Facing Death*. Lexington, Mass.: Free Press, 1990.

Sanders, Catherine. *Surviving Grief . . . And Learning to Live Again*. New York: John Wiley and Sons, 1992.

Schiff, Harriet Sarnoff. *Living Through Mourning: Finding Comfort and Hope When a Loved One Has Died*. New York: Viking Penguin, 1986.

Schuller, Robert. *Life's Not Fair but God Is Good*. Nashville, Tenn.: Thomas Nelson Publishers, 1991.

Staudacher, Carol. *Beyond Grief: A Guide for Recovering from the Death of a Loved One*. Oakland, Calif.: New Harbinger Publications, 1987.

Yalom, Irvin D. *Love's Executioner*. New York: HarperCollins, 1989.